SAVED BY CHANCE...

Part One of the Fisher of Men Series

by Frank Parks

In memory of my sister, Angel

Saved by Chance...

Trilogy Christian Publishers
A Wholly Owned Subsidiary of Trinity Broadcasting Network
2442 Michelle Drive, Tustin, CA 92780

Copyright © 2025 by Frank Parks

Scripture quotations marked HCSB are taken from the Holman Christian Standard Bible®, Copyright © 1999, 2000, 2002, 2003 by Holman Bible Publishers. Used by permission.

Scripture quotations marked NIV are taken from the Holy Bible, New International Version®, NIV®. Copyright © 1973, 1978, 1984, 2011 by Biblica, Inc.™ Used by permission of Zondervan. All rights reserved worldwide. www.zondervan.com. The "NIV" and "New International Version" are trademarks registered in the United States Patent and Trademark Office by Biblica, Inc.™

All rights reserved, including the right to reproduce this book or portions thereof in any form whatsoever. For information, address Trilogy Christian Publishing Rights Department, 2442 Michelle Drive, Tustin, CA 92780.

Trilogy Christian Publishing/TBN and colophon are trademarks of Trinity Broadcasting Network.

For information about special discounts for bulk purchases, please contact Trilogy Christian Publishing.

Trilogy Disclaimer: The views and content expressed in this book are those of the author and may not necessarily reflect the views and doctrine of Trilogy Christian Publishing or the Trinity Broadcasting Network.

10 9 8 7 6 5 4 3 2 1
Library of Congress Cataloging-in-Publication Data is available.

ISBN 979-8-89041-973-6
ISBN 979-8-89041-974-3 (ebook)

TABLE OF CONTENTS

Chapter 1: Rough Start 5
Chapter 2: Scrapper 11
Chapter 3: Experimentation 17
Chapter 4: Fight for Your Right 23
Chapter 5: Close Calls 31
Chapter 6: Spiritual Awakening 39
Chapter 7: Freedom in Prison 47
Chapter 8: Fresh Start 53
Chapter 9: Life with LoveLeigh 61
Chapter 10: Frank's Island 89
Chapter 11: Surrender 105
Chapter 12: Becoming a Fisherman 139
Chapter 13: Going Deeper 149
Chapter 14: Reel 'Em In 161
Chapter 14: Fisher of Men Foundation 167
Chapter 15: Nothing but God 175
Chapter 16: Building an Ark 181

CHAPTER 1:

Rough Start

It was Friday, the 13th of October, 1989, and since I believed in luck and that I did not have any, I thought today would be a good day to kill myself.

I was nineteen years old and strung out, getting high and drunk every day. I had been using heavily for a while, and on this night, I had run out of drugs, booze, and money, but mostly, I had run out of hope. I always messed up everything in my life, so what was the point of it all? I was a lost cause, ex-convict, liar, thief, cheat, drunk, addict, and baby killer, and I did not deserve to live. I was on my way to the medicine cabinet to get all the pills I could take. I just wanted to go to sleep and never wake up, but I stopped to look in the mirror in my room and started talking to myself. Out loud, I said, "What is wrong with you, Frank? Why do you want to kill yourself?"

How did I end up in such a mess? I was born on the Fourth of July, 1970. My mom was a seventeen-year-old flower child, one of six in a blended family, a dysfunctional Brady Bunch. My poppop had two kids from a previous marriage, and my mommom had one. My mom was their first child together, or so we were led to believe until recently. Upon obtaining a copy of her birth certificate, my mom was slightly surprised to see another man's name where her father's should have been. When asked about this other man, my mommom claimed she had made up a name in an attempt to get even with my poppop after a fight. To say my mommom was a trip is an absolute understatement.

My mom was single until I was seven, so we spent a lot of time with Mommom and Poppop. They spoiled me rotten and gave me anything I wanted, including sips of their gin and tonics. Some of my first memories revolve around drinking alcohol. It may sound strange, but I was unaware of the absence of my father for a long time. I never saw him or even heard about him until I was about four years old. It was just me, my sister, mom, mommom, poppop, and all my aunts, uncles, and cousins. There were so many of us that a missing dad went unnoticed. My poppop took me to get my first haircut, and my mommom bought me Matchbox cars. They took me camping and fishing, and life seemed pretty good.

I still remember the day my mom told us that our dad was coming for a visit. He was Frank Sr., and I was little Frankie. He pulled up in a VW bus, the side door opened, and he rolled out in a cloud of smoke. He had long hair and a scruffy beard. He looked like Jesus in Army fatigues. I was so excited that I ran to his arms and felt an instant connection. He scooped me up and carried me into the house. I still remember how he smelled. It was a mix of marijuana and patchouli oil. My mom just glared at both of us and immediately started to berate him, probably because he was high. She had a few choice words; he replied in kind, put me down, and left. I did not see him again until I was in the third grade.

Mom got a job at an apartment complex, so we moved out of Mommom and Poppop's. My sister, Angel, and I would play on the playground with no supervision at a very young age. We rode our Big Wheels around the complex. One time, two little boys tried to take her Big Wheel, and I beat the crap out of them. I was around four years old and had never been in a fight, but I just snapped. Punching and kicking them, I felt like a little Bruce Lee. I had watched him on TV and just assumed this was okay. When they went home bleeding and crying, they came back with their mom.

I was simply trying to be a hero by coming to my sister's rescue, but I was clearly out of control even at four years old.

My mom tried to keep me from hitting people, but at that point, the monster had been unleashed. She also "gave me something to cry about" when I would get out of line. I am sure I deserved every spanking, but I didn't think it was fair that I could get a whooping and wasn't allowed to dish them out! Still spending a lot of time at Mommom's and Poppop's, I eventually saw my Poppop snap and realized that a bad temper ran in the family. He threw the butter dish into a bowl of tomato soup and yelled at my mommom for something I don't remember. They fought all night while my sister and I stayed in our room and cried. This memory breaks my heart, as my anger has been out of control too many times to count. I am grateful that I do not live that way today.

As fighting continued throughout my childhood, so did partying. There was a drum set in the living room, and a band would come over on weekends for ragers at Mommom's and Poppop's. At three, four, and five years old, I would take sips of everyone's drinks until I was hammered. They would even get our dog drunk. One time, our dog ran into the fridge and knocked himself out. I was drunk and laughed so hard that we both passed out on the kitchen floor. I was a baby lush and would stumble around and get laughed at by everyone. Looking back now, I can see it was insane to let a toddler drink, but that was normal in my family.

When I was five, Mom left her hometown and moved an hour south. She worked at another apartment complex, and my sister and I shared a room. I started kindergarten and went to daycare after school, where the fighting continued. Once, at daycare, a boy took a toy from me on the playground, and I beat him up. My mom was called in, and I was warned that if I got into any more trouble, I would get kicked out. Shortly after this incident, a little girl pulled my sister's hair and made her cry. I didn't say stop or give any warning; I just punched her in the nose. Blood went everywhere, and I was kicked out of daycare. My mom was at a loss as to what to do with me, so she gave me a key to our apartment to wear around my neck; I was the definition of a latchkey kid in kindergarten.

Around this time, Mom started dating a guy named Bob. I thought he was rich. He would buy my sister and me whatever we wanted. He had about seven cars, including several Corvettes, a couple of MGs (which my mom would drive), and a Cadillac or Lincoln. He was a lot of fun and gave me a lot of attention. One day, he took me to work with him, and we went to a construction site. He took me to meet a guy who was not happy to see either of us there. I remember Bob telling him to be nice in front of "the kid." The man we went to see had some choice words and told Bob that he was lucky I was there.

Not long after this, I was walking to school late, as usual, when a police officer asked if I wanted a ride to get to school faster. I thought this was cool; the cop knew my name, and his car was pretty neat, so I rode with him to school. Now, I was often late to school because I set my own alarm and got myself ready. My mom worked late, so I stayed up as long as I wanted. She taught me how to do everything myself, including fixing my own breakfast. There were times when there was not a lot of food in the house, but we usually had all the *Os*—Cheerios, Spaghetti-Os, and Oreos. That night, when I told her about my ride to school, she was very upset. Her reaction was not what I was expecting at all. She berated me and told me never to get in a car with a stranger. When I tried to argue that the police were "good guys," she claimed that anyone could dress up like a policeman, even a kidnapper.

Another day after school, I came home, and Mom was there, which was very unusual. She had a black eye and was crying. She told me she had just hit her face on a door and would not be going to work. Shortly after this, Mom and Bob broke up, and he asked to take me and my sister to live with him. While they were fighting, my mom told Bob that we would never live with him. He convinced her to let us decide and put us in the middle of the room. I had no idea at the time that Bob was a married man living a double life. My aunt also thought he was dealing drugs, which would explain the ride in the police car and the visit to the construction site. As a kid without a clue, I just thought he was a lot of fun and bought me whatever I wanted. My sister immediately ran to my mom, but I stood in the middle, questioning why Bob and I couldn't live together. My mom started screaming, "Get over here right now!" The longer I hesitated, the more upset she became, and she started crying. I eventually went to her, but I still wanted a dad.

CHAPTER 2:

Scrapper

I tried to make the best of life playing with my friends in the apartment complex, but somehow, I would always get into a fight and blow up over things I can't even remember. I was a cute little blond-haired, blue-eyed Eddie Haskell-like kid. People would see me as harmless until things didn't go my way, then I would explode.

In first grade, there was a boy named Gilbert in my class. He was a bully, was supposed to be in third grade, and had a redhead bigger than everyone else. We were all afraid of him. He pushed me off of the slide at recess, and I went off like a rocket, hitting and kicking him. The teachers pulled me off of him while I was slamming his head on the pavement. I had him by the hair, and his forehead was bloody. Most of the time, I was a fun-loving kid, but when the trigger was tripped, I was a little monster. I ended up in the principal's office and got a warning about the paddle and how many days I had been late to school. We had a parent-teacher conference, and I straightened up for a while.

I think it was between first and second grade when my mom started dating a new guy. They met at the bar where my mom was working as a cocktail waitress. He gave her big tips, and pretty soon, they were serious. My mom took us to meet him for the first time, and we were sent outside to play. I came back inside for something and saw them making out on the couch. In the awkwardness, they gave me a look like, "Leave us alone." I felt as if I was on the receiving end of that look for much of my childhood. They married, and I eventually started calling him Dad. He coached me in Little League for a year. I had a good time playing baseball, but he soon lost interest and began dropping me off at practice. I often felt like I was in last place when it came to work, their friends, and their social life.

For this reason, I couldn't even appreciate the good things they did for me. We would take vacations to go skiing and spend time with our cousins on the water, where I learned to water ski and kneeboard. We went fishing and crabbing and drove a go-cart. It was an awesome place, but as I got older, I lost appreciation for going there, as well. I had no sense of fulfillment and remained wholly discontent.

I always had this self-fulfilling feeling that I was just a nuisance. I was always getting in trouble, getting into fights, picking on my sister, and skipping school. I even got caught shoplifting in the second grade; I asked for a pack of gum and was told no, so I took it. Later, my mom found it in the laundry and made me take it back to the store. It was agreed that I would come sweep the store for a week as restitution. I went once and told my mom I went the rest of the time, but I played with my friends instead and continued to steal.

At a very young age, girls began to pay attention to me. In first grade, I started getting love notes and was chased by a mob of girls on the playground. They held me down and kissed me. I acted like I was resisting, but I loved the attention. A friend of my mother's had a beautiful daughter who was a year older than me. She spent the night with me and my sister and taught me things a third-grader should not know, like how to French kiss and fondle. I did not have a conscience about many things, but my sister was with us and wanted to be involved as well. I remember telling her that she was not old enough. As much as I picked on her, I was always very protective of her. If anyone messed with her, a beating was coming.

The next night, when it was time for bed, I tried to give my mom a French kiss, and thankfully, she stopped me. She got upset, and when I told her where I learned this, there were no more sleep overs for a while. Another time, while her friend with the beautiful daughter was visiting, I went streaking through the house laughing like a maniac. I would do anything for attention. I had my first girlfriend in the second grade, and she broke up with me because I kept grabbing her butt.

We moved to a new house and started a new school in third grade. That summer, I spent about a month with my grandparents, aunts, and uncles. One of my uncles was good friends with my biological father and asked if I wanted to see him. My sister didn't go, and now I suspect this was because we have different fathers. We went fishing with my uncle and cousin. They gave us beer, we smoked some weed, and I got to drive the truck. I thought it was awesome because I always wanted to be grown up and do whatever I wanted. I felt like a grown-up and told my sister all about my visit. She told my mom, and I did not get to see him or my uncle again.

My mom and new dad started the adoption process. Not only did our address change but so did my last name and everything about the way we lived. We had structure in the house. We went to bed early, got up for school on time, did our homework, and had dinner as a family more often. There was food in the fridge, and we seemed to have the perfect family. Even though this is what I needed, I hated it. I wanted to do what I wanted to do. I wanted to stay up late and skip school; I thought I knew it all. Even though my life had turned for the better, I had no sense of gratitude and held resentment toward my mom and new dad. I would lay in bed and wonder about my "real" dad.

As I began the third grade, my parents began to pursue the American Dream. My mom had gone from being a property manager and cocktail waitress to becoming a real estate agent. It was in the late '70s, and interest rates began to rise through the roof. There were lines at the gas pumps. My dad worked in management for a major manufacturing company.

We moved to a townhouse community with a pool and a tennis court across the street. There were a lot of kids in the neighborhood, and we would play outside every day. Football, baseball, basketball, street hockey, swimming, tennis, hide-and-seek, kickball, and wiffleball. It did not matter what the sport was; we were playing and competing, and I hated to lose. There was an older kid in the neighborhood who dominated the activities, and as someone who did not like being told what to do, I protested often. I would often get beaten during the game, and being a sore loser would lead to another beating by this kid, who was quite a bully.

Eventually, I got tired of the beatings. During a wiffleball game, after getting punched one too many times, I took the bat and beat him to a pile on the ground. Just like the fight in first grade, I went from being bullied to becoming one. All of a sudden, people were afraid to mess with me. My temper was always a problem and would get me in trouble over and over. Often, the games in the neighborhood would end in a fight. It did not matter who it was, girl or boy, younger or older, bigger or smaller: I would fight anyone who disagreed with me. I would rarely lose a fight, and when I did, I would cheat or fight dirty to get even.

    The structure in the house helped my schoolwork, and I started getting good grades. In fourth grade, I made all As and a B, but when I got to middle school, my grades started slipping.

CHAPTER 3:

Experimentation

In fifth grade, we had an assembly where police officers came to tell us about the dangers of drugs. We learned that marijuana smelled like burnt rope and could be laced with other drugs. We were told that LSD was being given out to little kids. We were also warned about cocaine and alcohol. For our homework, we were given an information package to take home to our parents and discuss.

Considering their negative reaction to the fishing trip with my biological father, I was surprised to hear their response to this information. After a very serious discussion, they informed me that if I ever became curious about drugs, I was to come to them. They knew where to get "safe drugs," which confused the hell out of me. We were told at school by the police that drugs were always bad. My parents told me that only some of them were bad, and they knew better.

The parties continued at our home, and sixth grade was when I began drinking alcohol on a regular basis. The neighborhood kids and I would mix up a concoction we called a "suicide." We would take a soda bottle and fill it with a little bit of each bottle in the liquor cabinet. We were home alone often, and our liquor cabinet was always full. We would regularly get wasted after school and pass out early.

My grades were slipping badly, and I started to change them on the report card so I would not get into trouble. I would change a D or F to a B. We started sneaking out at night to terrorize the neighborhood. We worked as pool checkers at the neighborhood pool and left the clubhouse open. There was a huge box of toilet paper that ended up all over the neighborhood trees, cars, and houses. We would throw eggs, rocks, and pinecones at cars and houses. When we finally got caught, my behind was kicked up the stairs!

We were a thorn in the side of the president of the homeowners association. We would play football and baseball in the common areas and destroy the grass and landscaping. He would plant trees, and we would tear them out; he would plant bigger trees, and we would sneak out and cut them down. One night, we slept out in tents with our parents' permission. We let the air out of the tires of his car, and one of my friends took a dump on the hood; needless to say, we got in some trouble for that one. That did not stop us, however. When we were grounded, we would just sneak out late at night, wreak havoc on the neighborhood, and then sleep during school.

During these days, I would pick on my sister all the time. She would get upset with me, and I would shove her by the head while shouting, "You're healed!" One time, while we were fighting, she tried to kick me while wearing a nightgown. When her leg came forward, the gown stopped her leg and pulled her back leg out from under her, and she went flying onto her backside. We both just cracked up. She was a good sport most of the time, but I was relentless. It was alright for me to pick on her, but God forbid if anyone else did. I was always looking for an excuse to fight, so anyone who messed with my sister had to deal with my terrorism.

During middle school, my fighting shifted from the playground to wherever my jealousy took control. As it had been in elementary school, I always had a different girlfriend. Usually, girls broke up with me because I was obnoxious. Whoever they would date next, I would harass and embarrass them until they would fight. I fought on the school bus, in the classroom, and in the lunchroom, bathroom, and hallway.

The summer before eighth grade, my parents threw a pool party for me. It was great; all the cool kids came, and I hooked up with a few girls. I always tried to play the field, but it did not work out very well. No matter how many relationships I had, I always ended up alone. I was always cheating on my girlfriends; therefore, I was always jealous. Usually, it ended in a fight with the next boyfriend.

Every time I got in trouble, I would decide to straighten up and do good for a while, but that never lasted long. Finally, at the beginning of eighth grade, my temper finally brought consequences. While playing a football game in the neighborhood, a girl came with water balloons. I hated her, but the truth is, we were a lot alike. She was always trying to get under our skin and wanted to play, but we would not include her. The water balloons were coming our way, and I went charging for hers. I grabbed her by the shirt, took the water balloon, and threw her on the ground. I ripped her shirt and started punching her. My friends stopped me, and we went back to our game. She went home crying, and the police called my house. My parents took me to the police station, and I was interrogated. After I shared what happened, I was fingerprinted and arrested. I felt like my life was ruined.

After I was arrested, my parents had a meeting with guidance counselors. After finding out how much I had been slacking off, they decided to send me to Catholic school. As I started my tenure there, I made new friends and instantly connected with the troublemakers, doing my best to lead the way. We had half-days on Wednesdays, which I loved. While my parents were working, we got drunk and started smoking cigarettes. While looking for matches in my house, we found a matchbox with half of a joint inside. My buddy wanted to smoke it, but I decided to look for more. We hit the jackpot and found a shoebox full of pot. Every Wednesday and weekend, we were drinking and getting high on Mom and Dad's stash.

The older I got, the more adventurous I became, raising Cain all over town, sneaking into girls' bedrooms, and playing dice on the strip where the drug dealers hung out. I started bringing some of my parents' weed and selling it. When I got to high school, news traveled fast. I was instantly popular with the seniors. They would pick me up, I would bring the weed, and they would get me alcohol and, eventually, cocaine. My midweek and weekend partying became more frequent. We started getting high and drinking every day before and during school. I would get girls wasted and take advantage of them. I started stealing my parents' car after they went to bed. It is a miracle that I never got caught or wrecked, as we would be high and drunk in the middle of the night, squealing tires and driving like maniacs.

While riding around in the car, I would sneak into girls' houses or break into community pools to go skinny dipping with whatever girl I could con into coming out with me. If I could not find a girl to hook up with, I would go out with friends just to wreak havoc on the town. I started frequenting "the strip," which was the street where all of the drug dealers hung out. I started playing quarters and rolling dice with them. I would stay out till the crack of dawn just about every night and then sneak back home just before my parents woke up. I would go to school and sleep through much of the day, only to do it again the next night.

I was always looking for a thrill. I was addicted to sex and pornography even before I was addicted to drugs. At the age of fifteen, I was arrested for stealing the Playboy with Madonna on the cover. Like every fifteen-year-old boy in 1985, I couldn't wait to see it. When I was arrested, I had a joint in my wallet. While I was in the back of the police car, I slipped my hands through the cuffs and stuck the joint between my butt cheeks. After going through the fingerprinting and processing, my parents picked me up. After being given a long lecture, I snuck out that night and smoked that same joint with some friends. They weren't really happy when I told them the joint spent a few hours in my butt crack... LOL. Things kept getting worse, and I just kept making bad decision after bad decision. I believed in luck and that I didn't have any. I just kept trying to escape my misery through self-medicating. I believed the lie that drugs and alcohol made me feel better. While I temporarily got some relief, the long-term effects were just more misery.

In high school, I started playing soccer and could run forever. I did not have a lot of skill, but in my annoying way,

I could pester the best player on any team by outrunning them and getting in their way. My parents were busy doing their thing, and I was doing mine. They came to two games throughout my entire high school career. I started taking speed before the games and would often get carded for my aggressive play. I also had some success making varsity as a sophomore and scoring two goals as a defender. I made all-conference my junior year, in spite of my drug use. If I knew where to get steroids, I would have taken them. Cheating to win was not a problem for me because I had no conscience.

In short, I terrorized my teachers and classmates.

CHAPTER 4:

Fight for Your Right

Finally, I had my driver's license and could drive legally. It was 1986, and the Beastie Boys came out with my theme song, "You Gotta Fight for Your Right to Party." We were "Raising Hell" with Run DMC. Looking back now, I think my parents were crazy for letting me get my license and drive their car. I had a fender bender the first night I drove legally while trying to back out of a driveway at a crowded party. I wanted to take some friends for a ride, so we kept going, anyway, to a curvy road. I was going eighty-plus miles per hour around a hairpin curve, and the car spun out of control. We did about five complete 360s and stopped in the middle of the road without a scratch on us. At that time in my life, I still did not consider myself lucky. Of course, I had been drinking and getting high, and we all realized that we could have died, but I didn't really care. Every time something good would happen to me, it was followed up by something worse. I was losing the will to live.

Before the end of my junior year, the private Catholic school I was attending made an announcement that they were closing down. I still feel somewhat responsible, as I did nothing to make it a good environment. My parents realized that they were wasting their money on the private school tuition, and since the school was closing anyway, they sent me back to public school. My first week there, I cut in the lunch line, and a big kid challenged me. I ran my mouth, and we met after school for a showdown. I wrestled for a little bit in middle school, so I went for a takedown. I woke up with my nose broken and teeth missing. Not only was the guy big, but he was also six feet four inches tall and knew karate. A spectator stopped him when I had enough. I woke up cursing him with a lisp because my teeth were gone. I went straight to the dentist and got new teeth. I had just gotten my braces off. My parents were sick over it, and so was I. My nose was fixed shortly after, only to get broken several more times, playing soccer and getting in fights.

The summer before my senior year, I met a girl who liked sex as much as I did. I snuck out every night and snuck into her bedroom. She did not like me doing drugs, so I just drank with her.

My parents started going away every weekend and leaving me and my sister home alone. One day, my sister came home from school and thought the house was on fire because there was so much smoke coming from the basement. Another weekend, we had a party with so many people that you could barely fit in the townhouse. I had very thoughtfully taken everything that could be broken and locked it in my parents' bedroom. The police showed up, and someone started to open the door. I went running to the door and dove to close it in the face of the police officer. He knocked on the door with his nightstick for what seemed like an hour. We sat quietly and waited for them to leave.

This was the first time since I started smoking pot that I tried to give it up. I did not want to stop but gave it a try for a little while. Drinking was fun but not the high I was looking for. I always wanted a bigger, better buzz. After several months of not using drugs, I eventually got high again, and it felt so good I regretted quitting at all. I thought pot made everything better, even sex and drinking. In my mind, it was the cure for everything.

During my senior year, I only had to go to school for a half day because I had enough credits to graduate. I would go to work at the restaurant where I had access to alcohol and could get high and eat. One day, while skipping school, my buddies and I were in my parents' hot tub, drinking beers and smoking weed. My mom came home from work and caught us red-handed. After everyone left, she confronted me about stealing her stash. She told me she was going to tell my dad, and we would take care of it when he got home. I did not wait till they got home. I packed a bag and left home for a couple of weeks. I heard the police were looking for me, but I went to a high school dance anyway. I stayed with some girls in a college in my hometown, partied the whole time, and skipped school until my parents left town.

I decided to go home when my mommom came to stay for a while. I could do no wrong in her eyes, and I knew she would look out for me when my parents got back. When they got home, my dad was covered in hives because he was so upset about me being gone. We tried to work things out, but both of us were more interested in partying than doing the right thing. We had some family counseling sessions, but things never changed. I went to counseling by myself but never took it seriously and just quit going.

Things started to go downhill pretty quickly after I ran away that first time. A couple of weeks later, two of my neighborhood friends broke into our home to steal the shoebox full of weed. They did not realize that I had just been caught dipping in the stash, and it had been moved. I became the target of the police investigation as I was taken to the basement, where the kids kicked in the window. My parents and the police knew that I had information about who broke into the house. The police officer threatened to charge me with conspiracy if I did not tell him who did it and why. Since I already had a record, it would not be hard to pin me with the crime. He really wanted to know what they were looking for, so I told him the truth about the shoebox. He backed off immediately and went to speak to my parents. He never told them what I shared with him, but they were not happy when I told them what I said to the detective. Ironically, the shoebox was moved to the ceiling of the basement, literally right over our heads, while I was being interrogated. Once I found the weed again, it was back to stealing as usual. The more I drank and used, the more trouble I got into, but I always thought I was just unlucky. I never considered that my addictions and poor decisions were the reasons I kept getting in trouble.

During this period, I was spending most of my time at my girlfriend's house. Her mom and stepdad really liked me. My girlfriend was a cheerleader, and they would come to my soccer games. I had high hopes after my junior year, but the new school and new coach did not give me a fair shot. All of the partying and my bad reputation did not help my cause, either. I would get amped up before the games with most of the other seniors, and we often found ourselves sitting on the bench. The team was losing badly, and as the season went on, I became more discouraged and started using more heavily. My parents came to the last game of my career and left before I even got in the game. It was senior night and only the second game they had ever been to see. We were losing nine to zero to our arch-rivals. The seniors were put in at the end of the game; we played like maniacs. The game ended nine to one after I got a yellow card for taking out one of their best players. After the game, the coach called me out in front of the team. I threw my jersey at him and told him I quit. Later that night, a group of us went to his house, flattened his tires, and soaped his windows with "9-1 loser" written all over his truck.

A couple of weeks later, the same group of hooligans and I were at a party in rival territory. It was a beautiful waterfront property with a hot tub and nice furniture everywhere. We were standing in the dining room playing quarters, and someone was leaning on the china cabinet. It came crashing down on the table. The kid who was having the party came in as we were picking up the cabinet. He started yelling at us to leave, and we tried to explain that we were just helping clean up the mess. He said he was calling the cops, so we went off and started trashing the house. There were dishes flying. I grabbed a hammer from the kitchen drawer and started smashing walls and mirrors. We threw the keg in the hot tub and then started looting the house. While the kid was chasing people out, we were going through the parents' bedroom. One of my friends found a gun, and we took it, along with some jewelry and other valuables. As we were leaving the house, the kid whose parents owned the house we just looted shot a gun in the air right behind my head. We then left in a hurry.

A few days later, we were all arrested as the stolen gun was found by the father of the kid we had trusted to keep it in a safe place. He turned all of us in, and we found out that the gun and the house we trashed belonged to a state trooper; this turned out to be a blessing in disguise, as the trooper did not want the publicity, either. My girlfriend's mom worked for a judge, and we all got off scot-free. This was the third time I was arrested with no real consequences, and I was getting used to the routine; I still hadn't seen a jail cell.

My dad came to pick me up from the police station, and a fight ensued. I lost my mind and started kicking and screaming that he was not going to hit me anymore. Even though I deserved every bit of discipline, I was out of control. He told me to get my things and get out. I packed up everything I could carry and left. He chased after me, and I outran him, loaded with backpacks and duffle bags. I was ready to go and could not wait to get out. I went to stay with my girlfriend for a little while. My mom came to talk to me and said that I could no longer come home. I was only going to be around for a few more months, anyway, but she had to spend the rest of her life with my father. They offered to help me get my own apartment, so I moved into a one-room efficiency by the college. I thought this was great, as I could finally do whatever I wanted. I would go to school sometimes, go to work every day, make enough tip money to buy some weed and a bottle, and party every night.

One of my co-workers at the restaurant asked me to check out some stuff for him. He had some coke and wanted to know if it was good or not. After I tested it for him, he started supplying me and all of my friends. He was the starting point guard for the varsity basketball team. I began to sell and use coke on a regular basis.

It wasn't long before several of my suppliers were busted for dealing. I came close, myself, one night as we were making a run to the beach to sell some bags. We sold a good amount but still had a lot left and got pulled over. We had been drinking, getting high, doing coke, and selling all day. We were pulled over as we were about to sell the rest of our bags. Two white guys and two black guys in a Mercedes on the strip stood out like a sore thumb. My best friend at the time handed me the bags of coke as the cop approached the car. When the cop asked where we had been, I told him we were working at the beach all day. I can't believe he let us go.

I still didn't feel lucky.

CHAPTER 5:
Close Calls

The apartment by the college was still great. We had parties every night, and college girls came over all the time. The drug dealing was going well enough to use as much as I wanted, but because I was using so much, I never had a lot of money for very long.

It was getting close to Christmas when my number was finally up. I went to school, and my dad saw me get dropped off. We left after homeroom, as we often did. Dad saw the car that dropped me off at my apartment and thought we were inside when we were actually a few doors down, skipping school at a friend's house. I thought my dad would just come and go when no one answered, but I had left a cassette tape playing when I went to school. He thought the guy who dropped me off was in the apartment with the music going, so he called the landlord and the police. When they opened the door, there was everything but the drugs. I had left the apartment a mess from the night before. We had been cutting bags of coke on a mirror, and the beer bong and the weed bong were left out. We had the drugs with us, so there was nothing in the house other than marijuana seeds, but I was arrested again for drug paraphernalia and maintaining a dwelling for the use and distribution of illegal drugs.

My parents bailed me out again and actually got an attorney to help get me off the charges. They kept giving me chance after chance and bailing me out time after time while I blamed them for having drugs in their house and setting a bad example. It was dysfunction at its finest. Meanwhile, my sister grew up in the same house and never once got arrested. I was such an ungrateful, lousy human being and did not see it at all. I just thought this is what people did. Everyone I hung out with partied hard, and if they did not, I thought they were missing out.

The apartment life was over for a while, and I moved back in with my parents. I set up shop in the basement. There was an outside door, and I could just come and go as I pleased. Being home did not slow down my partying in the least. My parents were gone all the time, either working, traveling, or out at the bars, so I did whatever I wanted. They spent a lot of weekends out of town, as well, so I could have friends over and continue to get high. I was still dipping in their stash, as well.

When I moved back home, the stash was moved, but I found it; one of my drug-using and dealing friends who knew where it used to be broke into our house on a rare day while I was at school. He did not find the shoebox full of weed, but my parents knew one of my friends had something to do with it. Needless to say, they were pretty upset, but because of them smoking weed and drinking, I believe they kept enabling me out of guilt.

As graduation approached, I was failing a required course for the second time and slept through most of the class most of the time. I needed an A on the final exam to graduate. The teacher finally gave me a detention for sleeping, and when I showed up to his class after school, he was not there, but the final exams from the prior semester were in his file cabinet. I stole the exam with the highest score I could find, and now I just had to hope that the test would be the same as the first semester. It was a multiple-choice test, and I wrote all of the answers on my hand and even marked the wrong ones. When I showed up on the last day to see my score, the teacher asked me, "How did you cheat?" I replied, "I took the class two times and got the highest score. How could I have cheated?" He knew I was lying, but I think the whole staff was glad to see me go.

Graduation day finally came, and I was so happy as I hated school and was so glad to be done. I just wanted to make money and party. As we were walking from the gym to the stadium for graduation, I was smoking a joint with one of my boys from the strip. People kept looking around, wondering where the smoke was coming from as we kept moving around in the line. Everyone was dressed alike in our cap and gowns, so we just kept moving and did not get caught.

Shortly after graduation, I moved into an apartment near the college once again. I was not on the lease, and the roommates were college students who were away for the summer. I had the place to myself, and we got high every night. We would listen to Steve Miller Band's "Fly Like an Eagle" and smoke, drink, and snort anything we could get our hands on. We got so wasted that one night, one of my friends pooped his pants!

This was an old house with bad water pressure. You could turn the faucet halfway off, and the water would stop running. Then, after the pressure built back up, it would come back on again. We left for the beach, and the water came back on, filled up the sink full of dirty dishes, and overflowed to the apartment downstairs. The landlord came in and saw the mess we had left, as well as the bong, and I was told I could not stay in the apartment because I was not on the lease. After that, I rigged up a string on a rock and would not answer the door unless someone pulled the string. We would be so high that when the rock would move, we would all cheer. We thought it was hilarious. One night, a guy just walked into the apartment. We did not know who it was, but he wanted to get high with us. He did not seem to inhale when he was smoking, and we swore it was a cop. We took him into the kitchen, frisked him, and made him leave because we were so paranoid.

I moved from that apartment to another one with some college girls, and my drug use got more intense. We started traveling to Philly to buy coke. We were selling it just to use more, buy more, an endless cycle. One night, I was so high on coke that I was afraid to move because I thought my heart would explode. My drinking had increased from a fifth a day to buying half-gallons. Near the end of my drinking, I could almost finish a half gallon, but I would invariably end up on the floor lying in my own puke. I remember several nights in a row lying on the floor while people came in and laughed at me, saying, "*Man*, he is wasted!" I couldn't get off the floor, no matter how hard I tried. I would just lie there in my puke until the next day and swear I would not do that again, only to go get another half-gallon the next night.

Another night at this place, one of my friends brought some weed over, and we were letting girls in and getting high and drunk. Then, a bunch of guys came over whom we did not let in—more girls and booze and weed for us. There were about five or six of them and only two of us, and they kept yelling at us for not letting them in and challenging us to come outside while shouting profanity and racial slurs. I was often called "Oreo Cookie" or "Salt and Pepper" because I had many Black friends. We were mad but did not fight because the numbers were not in our favor, and my friend just had his wisdom teeth out.

A week or two later, I was at another party at someone else's house. These guys showed up again, and I was by myself. They were a punk rock skinhead crew. One of them had his hair cut like devil horns. They were screaming at me to go outside, and the owner of the house was just begging them not to fight in his house. These guys were just waiting for me to go outside to jump me when my friend showed up with the Del State basketball team. My friend pointed out the kid who called him the N-word, and the basketball team chased him out of the house. It turned out to be a great night, and for the first time in a long time, I felt lucky for a change.

In this same house, I had gotten a girlfriend high, and she freaked out and called her brother. He and a bunch of his friends showed up, and they watched him beat the crap out of me while I begged for mercy. He thought I took advantage of her and gave her something to knock her out. I finally convinced him it was just some really good weed, and she would be okay. I was very manipulative, but if I could not convince a girl to have sex, I would just go "take matters into my own hands."

Girls would come over, and I would use them. My behavior was very risky, often sleeping with multiple girls on the same day. My addiction to sex was just as bad as my drug and alcohol addiction. Most nights, I would go back to my old girlfriend's house, sneak in, have sex, and sneak out. She had a new boyfriend, but I did not care. One night, I went to her house and challenged her boyfriend to come outside. Her dad did, instead. We got into a fight, and I got the better of him, only for the police to come and haul me away. I did not get arrested for that one, either, but I still did not feel lucky. While I was being driven away in the police car, my ex-girlfriend mouthed the words, "I love you." It was a pretty sick and twisted relationship. Once I got out of the police station, I went back to her house, snuck in, had sex, and left.

I kept going back every night, tossing stones up to her window. Eventually, she told me she was pregnant. Immediately, I selfishly thought of how there was no way I could take care of a child. I couldn't take care of myself. I asked how she knew it was mine, even though I knew in my heart that it was my baby. After all, she had a boyfriend. I told her to have an abortion and have him pay for it. She did, and I kept coming over to get what I wanted with no care for her feelings or the trauma she had been through. She would always try to cut me off, and I would always manipulate her. I was abusive, verbally and physically. I was a wretch in every sense of the word.

I am not sure how I ended up back at my parents' place, but I was living back in the basement with the back door. I would come and go as I pleased and was still partying out of control, chasing every high imaginable. A typical day looked like a bong hit, waiting tables, using and selling coke, and drinking at the restaurant. I would take my tips and buy another bag of weed and a bottle to get wrecked. I would continue to use coke so I could keep drinking and smoking weed without passing out. If there was some acid available, I would take that to keep the buzz going around the clock. I would try to have sex with every girl I could and would still go to my old girlfriend's place to finish off the day. I would sneak back out, go home, and get another bong hit to start the next day.

Around this time, I resorted to suicidal threats to guilt my old girlfriend into letting me sneak into her bedroom every night. I was a mess, and everything was overwhelming. I was still working but having a hard time even doing my job. At the end of a week-long acid trip, I finally had a meltdown. All of my friends, family, and co-workers were disgusted with me. I could not see the good in anything or anyone, and they could not see it in me, either. The truth is, there wasn't any.

After a week of using more than I ever had, suicidal thoughts became an obsession. I started to think about how I would kill myself. Finally, on Friday, the 13th of October 1989, I decided that I was tired of being unlucky, and there wasn't enough alcohol, drugs, sex, or money to fix what was wrong with me. Friday the 13th was a good day to die, and I should just end it all. Pills were the answer. I would just take all the pills I could find and not wake up. I began to walk to the medicine cabinet, and something stopped me…

CHAPTER 6:
Spiritual Awakening

For a moment, I looked in the mirror in my room and started talking to myself. Out loud, I said, "What is wrong with you, Frank? Why do you want to kill yourself?" I had a roof over my head, could walk and talk, could see and hear, had all my fingers and toes, could see and reason. I was not the smartest guy in the world, but I was not the dumbest, the richest or the poorest, the fastest or the slowest. All of a sudden, being average wasn't a bad thing. I began to think about how my mom had me when she was seventeen and how she could've had an abortion like my girlfriend did. For the first time in my life, I felt fortunate to be alive, and I had a little bit of gratitude and a whole lot of guilt.

I walked over to my bed, dropped to my knees, and began to pray. I broke into tears and begged for forgiveness. I pleaded with God to forgive me for being such a lousy person, for abusing drugs and alcohol, for mistreating myself and others, especially my girlfriend, for not taking responsibility for her pregnancy and encouraging her to get an abortion. I felt like a murderer, and when I asked God to forgive me for all of these things, especially for killing my baby, I felt peace and forgiveness come over me. It was warm and comforting... my whole body tingled. It was better than any high I had ever experienced. Something changed that night, and my doubts and desire to die were gone.

I jumped off the floor, excited to see what God had in store for my life. I had a joy and hope that I never felt before. There was no pastor or sermon, praise band, or church. There was just God and my broken soul, alone and pleading for redemption. From that moment on, I knew God was real, and no one could convince me otherwise. I no longer believed in luck but knew that God had a reason for everything. I was not alone and talking to myself. I started talking to Him and had a new purpose. I started a journey to figure out God's plan for my life. I could hardly sleep and spent much of the night praying.

At this point, I wish I could say that my life got better, but it did not. While I had taken a huge step forward and cheated death once again, I did not know what to do next. I was still an addict and had questions about why God made things the way He did. Why did He create drugs if we weren't supposed to use them? Why would He allow us to be born if He knew that we were going to suffer? I started seeking without a solid mentor in my life. No one I hung out with had a strong faith or even a little bit of sobriety, so I started asking questions to people who thought the answer was to party.

The next morning, I went to talk to my parents as they were going to Parents' Day with friends at a nearby college. When I questioned them as to why they were going when they did not have any kids there, their reply was something to the effect that I could be going there if I wasn't living in the basement doing nothing with my life. It was obvious they were disgusted with me, and for good reason. I realized that God had forgiven me, but they had not. They left in disgust, and then I called my grandmother to talk about my experience with God since my parents were not interested in anything I had to say. My mommom and I had a good talk, and she answered a lot of my questions about God and life, but there was one question that sent me in the wrong direction. I asked her, "If there was a God and He created everything, why did He create drugs?" Her reply was that drugs heal sick people.

While I now believed in God, I was still addicted to drugs. This answer gave me the justification I needed. I convinced myself that marijuana was the cure for the common cold. After all, I had not had a cold since I had been smoking pot. It also cured my hangover every morning. It was a miracle drug. I made it my mission to legalize all drugs and decided that by doing so, I could heal everyone. I attributed my spiritual awakening to being drug-induced. I tried to convince people to get high and believe in God, that He made drugs for us to use and they should be legal. I told everyone my plan to save the world while I stayed drunk and high for the next sixty days.

I was kicked out of the house again after berating my sister for judging me. She did not approve of my drug use or my manic behavior. One night, while waiting tables at the restaurant and sharing my new philosophy about drugs healing the world and bringing everyone closer to God, I was fired. I walked out with all of the money from my tables that night. The problem was that I was supposed to turn in the payments for the meals and keep my tips. I stole the $300 I was supposed to turn in and rented a video camera.

My plan was to leave town and travel across the country while filming our adventures, then take the film to a Hollywood producer. It was going to be a reality movie. The opening scene was me and my friend walking and talking about our plan. The second scene was his mom swinging at him while he was trying to film her. This friend had been using crack for some time, and his mom knew he had stolen the camera. The next day, I left the camera with my friend and traded in my scooter for a car. I went to get insurance for the car and pretended to have the money. Once the card was typed up, I grabbed it off the agent's desk and ran out of the office.

I went to the DMV to get tags. I'm not really sure why I cared so much about having insurance and tags, but I thought that would get us further because we were definitely getting pulled over. I distinctly remember praying constantly and asking God for His will to be done, but I was so addicted and manic—my thoughts and plans were as twisted as ever.

After I had spent the day getting everything ready to go, I went to pick up my buddy, who was supposed to be packing and holding the camera. When I got to his house, I said, "Are you ready to go?" He gave me a look of shame and said he couldn't go. I asked him where the camera was, and he told me he had returned it for the money. Then I asked him where the money was, and he admitted that he had smoked it…all of it. I was completely shocked that the crackhead thief, who was the only person who would be willing to go across the country on a crime spree in a fifteen-year-old Cutlass junker, would screw me. Man, what was I thinking?

So, I had no job, and the cops were looking for me again. I had a car and maybe $50 cash, so instead of Hollywood, I decided to go to New York. I went to see one of my old friends, whom I had heard was doing well in the movie business. When I got to his apartment, it was clear that he was not doing as well as people were saying, and he was doing gay porn. I had no morals, but I liked women only. After unpacking my car and staying the night, we both decided it would be best if I went home and turned myself in. I was still on probation, wanted for the $300 that my buddy smoked up, and really had no interest in gay porn.

I drove home, and the car started to rattle badly. I took it to a used car place to try to get the $300 to take back to the restaurant. I remember the owner offering me a couple hundred bucks. Then I told him the truth about me taking the money and needing $300 to pay back my debt. Wouldn't you know, it worked. He asked why I didn't tell him sooner and gave me all $300. God was working on my conscience. I started to be more honest and admit my mistakes.

After taking the money back, I had no money, no car, no job, and no place to live. All my clothes were in New York. My plan was really falling apart, but God's plan was coming together. I managed to get a few dollars together and went to the racetrack. I figured gambling might help me get some quick cash. I made a few safe bets and won a couple of bucks, only to lose it all on a hunch. I hadn't bathed for days, so I went to a friend's house to ask him to use his shower and borrow some clothes. This was a friend I had given rides to all over town until he got his license. He did let me clean up and gave me some clothes, but he told me I had to leave and I should go get some help.

I went to see my old girlfriend, but she wouldn't let me in. Every door was closed in my face. I went to my old school, where I knew how to break into the gym and slept up on the stage on the gym mats. There was morning basketball practice, and I just walked out without speaking to anyone. They just looked at me like there was something wrong with me, which there was. I went back the next night and slept in the choir loft at the Catholic church on the same property. The whole time, I just kept praying for God to show me what to do next. I was running out of places to go, feeling lost again. I manipulated my old girlfriend to let me back into her house with threats of suicide. We got into an argument, and I pretended to have cut my wrists with a knife and some ketchup. The next morning, I left her house and had to meet my probation officer. I started running and collapsed. My body was giving out, and I was only nineteen years old. I became a walking skeleton. I did not eat right and hardly slept. My probation officer told me I had a court date and that it did not look good for me.

I decided to go home, but my sister would not let me in. I told her I could kill someone, referring to myself. She would not open the door. It was two days before Christmas, and I was tired of being homeless, broke, hungry, hungover, and lost. I kicked open the door, and she ran out of the house crying. I looked under the tree to see if there were any presents for me. Of course, there were none, so I cleaned myself up, grabbed some of my old clothes, and fixed myself a sandwich. After I ate about half of it, the cops came in and took me away.

At the police station, I had on a Steelers sweatshirt, and one of the cops asked me if I liked football. When I said yes, he told me that in prison, you go in a tight end, you come out a wide receiver. I laughed and tried to play it cool, but I was petrified.

Then, they put me in a cell.

For the first time in my life, I saw the inside of a prison cell. I figured I would make my phone call, and someone would bail me out. They said I could only call my parents, and I refused. I argued, and they left me in the cell. I lay down and went to sleep. They woke me up in the middle of the night and put me in a squad car. When I asked where we were going, they told me prison. Not the cozy cell in the police station, I was going to the big house with the rapists and murderers, and I was terrified.

All of a sudden, I was on my way to Smyrna prison.

CHAPTER 7:

Freedom in Prison

I started to freak out and scream at the cop, and he just smiled and dragged me into the intake. He told me that everyone was sleeping, and if I continued to run my mouth and wake everyone up, I would definitely be "getting raped tonight." So, I shut up and went through the holding cell very quietly. It was very dimly lit, and there was steam everywhere. It was raining from the ceiling. It looked like I was in hell. This was worse than anything I had ever pictured. Even in the movies, prison was not this bad. I was strip-searched and sent to a bunk. I kept my back to the wall and stayed up all night. I found out the next morning there was a leaky pipe, and that was the reason for the steam and rain inside. Eventually, they fixed the pipe, and the sun came up. It was the day before Christmas, and I met a devout Muslim man who prayed before I left. *"Allahu Akbar… Allahu Akbar."* We spoke about God, and I remember him telling me that patience is the key to success.

I was still pretty tired and strung out. They took me to a hearing in family court. My mom and a judge were there. I lost it again. I told the judge that my mother was a terrible mother and deserved to be the one locked up. Also that there was only one judge, God almighty, and the judge was going to hell for judging me. What was I thinking? That was all he needed to hear to say, "Courts adjourned!" and send me back to prison to await sentencing.

No more holding cell; I went to pre-trial. They took my clothes and the only personal items I had and left me with my shoes because they were out of the prison issue sneakers. I was wearing black Rockports. I'm not sure why I had dress shoes on when they picked me up from my parents' house, but they were really nice. I remember everyone commenting on my shoes, and it seemed odd that everyone else had standard-issue plastic-soled sneakers. There, I met my new cellmate, Puerto Rican George. George was an expert in prison life. He would party all summer long, and then, when it got cold outside, he would get arrested so he could spend the winter months getting three hots and a cot. I was pretty strung out and skinny, only weighing about one hundred and twenty pounds. George said he would make sure nothing happened to me, and I told him that if he upheld his end, I would give him my shoes.

There were about forty cells on our tier—twenty down each side with a wide hallway—and one TV at the end of the hall by the guard station. The door at the other end went out to the yard, but since there was snow, we stayed inside. Other than meals and shower time, we got one hour out of our cell in the hall.

And so, my new routine began. We woke up to a guard clanging his nightstick on the bars, screaming, "Chow time!" Then, after we ate what can be best described as slop, the same guard would scream, "Lock 'em up," and we would sit in our cells until lunchtime.

Sometime that first day, a Gideon pastor brought pocket Bibles to all of the inmates. He handed me the Bible through the cell, and we talked for a few minutes. I shared with him some of my story and that I had just recently become a believer who thought God created drugs and they should be legal. He told me to read the book of John and pray about what God would want me to do with my life. I did what he said.

This may sound insane, but I found more peace on that Christmas in that jail cell, knowing God was with me, than all my years prior. There were no presents, no family, no tree, no Santa, but there was Jesus, and I knew God had me right where I needed to be.

I started reading, praying, and exercising. We had shower time before lockdown for the night. They would bring us fresh towels, and mine was ripped, barely wrapping around me. As I walked down the tier, they were catcalling, "Fresh meat!" George said not to worry because we were in pre-trial. If anyone did anything, they would get more time added. Now, if we were in the general population, it would be a different story. I was still concerned and carried a pencil in my pocket, just in case I had to shank somebody. I was scared of being raped, but George was true to his word, and no one messed with him or me.

One day, while George was on the tier watching TV, this guy came into our cell and demanded that I give him my shoes. I said, "No, I promised them to George." He replied, "Then you are gonna get raped, then!" as he was dropping his pants. I pushed him and ran out of the cell. He came out laughing and pulling up his pants. He said he was just messing with me, but I didn't think it was funny at all. The guy was in there for raping a woman in a department store bathroom. He had hid in the drop ceiling and waited for her.

I kept reading the Bible and putting on weight and muscle. One night, I was biting my nails, and my front tooth came out, the fake one from the fight when I was seventeen. After seeing my snaggle-toothed smile, George said I looked like I belonged in jail, and nobody would mess with me now!

After a couple of weeks, I was doing a thousand push-ups a day. There was nothing else to do, and the bigger I got, the less of a target I became. I probably put on twenty-five pounds of muscle in one month.

I had a couple of meetings with the sergeant who knew my parents. He said he had been talking to them about how I was doing, but I had no communication with anyone outside of the prison while I was waiting for my sentencing. My trial date was coming up, and George was getting transferred out. As promised, I gave him my shoes and wished him well. Right after he left, the rapist came by my cell to see if the shoes were gone. He shook my hand and said, "I am glad you did what you said you were going to do."

My next cellmate was a Christian who had been convicted of a drug charge in a school zone, so he was between federal prison trips. I still had not let go of the thought of drugs becoming legal, and he told me I was completely wrong. The more I read about Jesus, the more I reconsidered drug use, but even Jesus drank wine and turned water into wine. Typically, we would watch TV and play chess or cards during our free time, but one day, a group of guys got together to pray on the tier. All of a sudden, this one guy who looked like Jesus started speaking in tongues and took his clothes off. I quickly left because I thought something must be wrong with him! I had heard about people speaking in tongues, but this was the first time I had witnessed it. The speaking in tongues did not really freak me out as much as the dude taking off his clothes since he was apparently there for child molestation!

Another night on the tier, this goofy White guy and I had a breakdance contest. He was a big goofy dude with dumbo ears but could pop, lock, and drop it like a boss. It was pretty hilarious, and it was the most fun I had in prison. We played spades and chess often, as well.

I began to pray throughout the day and surrender to God's will. My anger began to leave, and I started thanking God for everything, even my missing tooth. Every night before bed, there would be chatter about everything, smack talk mostly.

The night before I had my court date, a skinny Black guy in the cell across from mine whipped out his junk and said, "Check this out." I busted out laughing and couldn't believe this little guy was hung like a horse. I figured if I was hung like that, I would be showing it off, too. When I told him to put that monster back in his pants, another big Black guy who was the queen of the tier commented that he couldn't wait to see it. I was rolling, but I was certainly glad to be leaving the next day.

I went back to court with a new attitude. I was clear-headed and healthy, and my probation officer could see a difference. He was amazed at the forty-day transformation. Prior to seeing me, he was going to recommend sentencing me to hard time in the general population until rehab, but after a short conversation, he changed his mind and recommended work release until I could go to rehab.

My transformation was just beginning. When I finally went to work release, I could have visitors. Aunt Kay, Uncle Jay, and Mommom came to see me. It was like the cavalry had arrived. I remember Aunt Kay leading the way, with Mommom and Uncle Jay coming right behind her. They had no idea how bad my active addiction had been, but as long as I wanted to stay sober, they were willing to help me.

After thirty days, I could get out on weekends, and they picked me up to stay with them.

CHAPTER 8:
Fresh Start

A nearby chicken plant was hiring and had a bus come to the work release center to pick us up. So, I spent my first week pulling skins off of chicken breasts. It was cold, smelly, and boring work. My hands were so swollen I couldn't wait to get another job.

A friend in work release told me there was a construction job available, so I rode with him to work and just started working. After I was there a couple of hours, the foreman came over to me and asked my name and had me fill out some paperwork. I then became a masonry laborer, toting blocks, setting up scaffolding, and mixing mortar. It was still cold outside, but it was way better than the chicken plant. I was getting paid to work out and took it as a challenge to do more every day. Eventually, I was able to get my laboring work done so I could start laying blocks. I was in the best shape of my life. I was grateful to have a job and be outside. After my time in pre-trial with twenty-three hours of lockdown, every bit of freedom I gained was appreciated. As I began to fill my day with work, I spent less time reading the Bible but still prayed throughout the day.

I would spend weekends at my aunt and uncle's house in Seaford. It was a small town about thirty miles from the prison and an hour from the ocean. They lived with my grandmother and their two children, an eleven-year-old son and a six-year-old daughter. I would help my uncle work on cars, and then we would play Nintendo with my cousin, staying up till all hours of the night. It became a new addiction for me, which was better than drugs and alcohol, but still not what God had planned for me. One weekend, we went to the beach as a family, and I stepped on a beautiful conch shell, which I picked up. We had a great time, and I just felt blessed.

A couple of weeks later, my cousin got in trouble for something and lost his cool. He shouted that he wished he was dead, and it broke my heart. I shared with him my story of wanting to kill myself at one time and how I was glad that I hadn't. If I killed myself, I wouldn't have gotten to be there with him and find that shell. I gave it to him and told him that you never know when you'll find a treasure. He seemed to get it and did better. It was the first time I felt that God had given me the opportunity to share my story to help someone. It gave me a sense of purpose, and I knew there was a reason God had let me go through such a trial.

I spent about six months in work release and just worked, exercised, prayed, and spent weekends with the family. I still did not hear anything from my mom, dad, and sister. My ex-girlfriend came to see me for my birthday on the Fourth of July, and we had sex in the woods behind my aunt's house; this was the last time we hooked up.

One day after work, we were playing spades in our room in work release, and my roommate said something smart to a guy from down the hall. He picked up my roommate and slammed him into the concrete wall. His head bounced off the wall, and he fell to the floor, completely unconscious. I was worried we would all get time added since it happened in our room. I was very close to leaving for rehab, and thankfully, the guy who did it admitted that he lost it and was sent back to general population.

One time, while I was in work release, I was praying and realized that I was making progress. I was getting myself up every day to go to work without doing drugs or drinking. I wrote a letter to my parents to make amends and to accept responsibility for the things I had done. I decided that I could no longer blame them for the mistakes I made. I was an adult, and it was time I started to act like one. It was very freeing to send that letter, and I felt as if I was on my way to a better life.

I was sober the whole time I was in prison and work release until the day before rehab. As the day approached, I became anxious and couldn't wait to leave. I started to become irritated with my co-workers and had a couple of reprimands on the job. One instance came when the head foreman called all of the subs together to give them hell for leaving trash on the jobsite, etc. He went on for ten or fifteen minutes, giving us a good cussing. When he finally quit, he asked if there were any questions, and I said, "Is it time for lunch yet?" Everyone laughed, and he didn't know who said it, so I thought I was in the clear. But my boss knew it was me and gave me some extra block toting. The day before I left for rehab, my boss was on a rampage, and I called him an a-hole under my breath. I definitely had short-timer syndrome.

My last day on the job was August 1, 1990. I was leaving for rehab the next day. It was a beautiful sunny day, but it felt like one hundred degrees after toting blocks and mixing mud all day. As usual, we piled in the van and went to the liquor store after work. The guys told me it was my last chance to have a beer and that I should have "one for the road." Since I was going to rehab the next day, I would never be allowed to drink again, and they chuckled. I agreed, and they gave me one last cold one. I cracked the can and chugged it in one shot. I always drank fast because I drank for effect. I did not ever really like the taste or enjoy sipping a beer or a drink. I wanted to slam as many as possible to get as wasted as possible in the shortest time possible. As I chugged the beer, I thought about having a few more, but I didn't. I wanted freedom more than I wanted a buzz. I went back to work release, packed my belongings, and went to rehab the next day.

On August 2, 1990, my new life began. I went to meet my counselor for the first time and thought everything was going well. I told her that I was done with drinking, drugs, and prison and ready for a fresh start. I told her that I was never going to drink or do drugs again, and she told me to stop lying to her and myself. In addition, if I didn't stop lying to her, she was going to have me sent back to jail.

I didn't understand why she was being so tough on me. I began to break down and just asked her to explain it to me. I really wanted to do better but did not know what to do. I stopped talking so much and listened.

She explained to me that we could never use the word *never* when talking about our future. We cannot control what happens tomorrow, and we cannot change what happened yesterday. All we can do is stay sober today and live one day at a time. I did not have to do anything more than I could do today. Tomorrow will work out if I do the right thing today.

I began to attend support groups, admitted my problems, and started making amends. I kept up my workout routine and learned how to box from my roommate. We both got in great shape and did everything we could do to stay on the right track. I felt like I was training to start the rest of my life. I did everything as perfectly as I could, even resisting temptation. There was a beautiful girl in the rehab who started rubbing my leg under a table. I moved away and told her that I was flattered, but I could not risk getting kicked out for hooking up. My cellmate in work release had come back from rehab after a week because he was caught having sex in the laundry room. I did not want to go backward.

While I was in rehab, I learned about a higher power and a God of my own understanding. I quit reading the Bible and started reading recovery literature. I learned about self-fulfilling prophecy and believed that I could determine my own destiny. I still believed in God, but I also realized that if I thought things would get better, they would. If I wanted to accomplish something and work toward a goal, I could achieve that goal. I was no longer under the rule of anyone, and I felt free. I felt like I had someone looking out for me, but I also believed what Henry Ford said: "If you think you can or you think you can't, you are right."

Once I surrendered, the twenty-eight-day program went smoothly. When I got out, I attended recovery group meetings in the evenings and got connected with other people in recovery. At my first meeting out of rehab, I was only twenty years old and not even old enough to legally drink. A man approached me after the meeting and shared that he would give his right arm to have gotten sober at my age. He was fifty or sixty years old. He said that if I stayed sober, I would be able to accomplish anything and live a life beyond my wildest dreams.

I listened intently and kept going to meetings. I prayed daily and looked at everything through new eyes. The fall colors were more vibrant, the snow was more beautiful, and the spring flowers were stunning. I thanked God every day for another day sober and free, and I learned how to live a boring life by myself without drugs, alcohol, or sex.

When I got home from rehab, I was blessed right away with another job. My aunt Kay's cousin Mark had recently opened a furniture store, and he gave me a job selling furniture. Mark is one of the most thoughtful people I have ever met. He always sent birthday cards and flowers; he attended funerals and genuinely cared about people. He showed me how to be considerate and think of others and was a great mentor to me. He was always the first one to arrive at the store and the last one to leave at night. He worked hard, and I appreciated him giving me an opportunity right out of rehab. Not many people would have taken that chance on a kid as screwed up as I was. I worked with Sandy and Rick. Rick was also in recovery, and we would have meetings every day at work. It was the perfect place for me. We had a lot of fun at the store, always playing jokes on each other.

Christmas was coming, and I realized the joy of giving. I bought a new stereo VCR for my aunt and uncle and the latest Nintendo for my cousins. I spent my whole month's paycheck on them, and it was the best feeling in the world. They said I gave them too much, but I could never repay them for giving me a chance and helping me get through work release and rehab.

One weekend, we rented the movie *Uncle Buck* starring John Candy. In the movie, Uncle Buck smoked, cursed, drank, gambled, and was a serious bowler. In spite of all of his shortcomings, he looked out for his nieces and nephew. He was an ass-kicking dude who bailed out his troubled teenage niece. My uncle cursed, smoked, and drank, and we bowled together in a weekly league. We stayed up late and played video games every night. After watching that movie, he was forever known as Uncle Buck. He was a family man; he took us camping and to amusement parks. He was an excellent mechanic, and we worked on cars together. He became my best friend and father figure.

Since I was getting my act together, I moved out of my aunt and uncle's house and moved into my own apartment that spring. My job was still going well, and I started to go back to college. I was taking classes and considered being a rehab counselor while working at the furniture store. I went on a few dates, but nothing serious. In the group I was attending, they said not to get into a serious relationship in the first year, so I stayed single and celibate. It was harder staying celibate than it was staying sober. Thank God for wet dreams, cold showers, and prayer. I felt as if I was faithful to God and sobriety and lived a pure life, I would be blessed with the right woman. I even changed my language. I tried not to curse and did my best to stay positive. I started encouraging others and telling jokes all the time.

That summer, I reconciled with my parents. I was paying my way when my mom and dad threw me a twenty-first birthday party. My friends all came and drank, and they were stunned that I did not. I was content and did not need to drink. After the party, I went back to my simple life, working in the furniture store, driving my car, and paying my bills in my one-bedroom apartment.

CHAPTER 9:
Life with LoveLeigh

After a year of sobriety and celibacy, I was getting a little discouraged that I hadn't met someone. I had high expectations; she had to be smart, beautiful, and faithful. I did not go to bars, and there was no internet, so meeting young women was not easy. I was going to my recovery group and knew I did not want to marry anyone as screwed up as I was.

One day, I went to the drug store where my aunt worked and saw this gorgeous young woman. Her blue eyes sparkled, she had curly hair that flowed down her back, and her dimpled smile was the brightest I had ever seen. *Beautiful... check.* After speaking to her for a minute, I knew she would be my wife, and I proposed to her on the spot. Just kidding, but I did know I would be pursuing her, though I did not know if she would let me catch her. I just asked her if she was new in the store because I had never seen her before. She told me she had worked there for a while but had been away at college and had just graduated. *Smart... check.*

I left the store, as there was another customer in line behind me, and immediately called my aunt to ask about this beautiful girl I had just met. Her name was Leigh Ann. My aunt told me that she had a serious boyfriend, was a Clemson graduate, and came from a great family. She didn't say it, but I could tell from her reply that she did not think I had a chance.

What I heard was, "Why would she want to go out with an ex-convict, drug-addicted, burnt-out loser?" That did not stop me. I kept going to the store to buy greeting cards and waiting for the line to be empty so I could talk to this amazing woman. Every time I spoke to her, I lost the nerve to ask her out, and someone would come up to the counter.

After stalking her for a couple of weeks, my aunt called to tell me that she had broken up with her boyfriend. *Single... check.*

I went to see her again and was going to ask her out, but there were customers, and she didn't seem like she was in a good mood. So, I left again and called the store when I got home. I asked her if she would like to go to the movies, and we set a date for the next night. I went to pick her up in my old car and drove down her parents' driveway. She lived in a nice home on the river, and I met her parents. It was obvious that my aunt was right: Leigh Ann did come from a good family. Her mom was very sweet and hospitable, and her dad was inquisitive. He wanted to know who was taking his daughter on a date.

There was an instant connection with her. The movie was okay, but the company was fabulous. We talked the whole way there and back. It was fall, and the World Series was on, so we went back to her parents' house and watched some of the game. When I decided to leave, she walked with me to my car. I turned to say goodbye, and she kissed me with her teeth. I wasn't expecting it, and our teeth banged together. I wasn't going to let the night end on that note, so I asked if we could try that again. The second kiss was incredible. She had the sweetest lips, and then I got down on one knee and proposed... Just kidding.

She did leave her jacket in my car—she says by accident, but I think it was her plan to see me again. So, we had another date. And then another. On our third date, I thought I would tell her about my past. So, I told her the whole wretched story. After the shock wore off her face, she asked me how many times I was arrested and how long I was sober. After our date, I thought, *If she goes out with me again, she is a keeper.* She did go out with me again. *Faithful… check.*

We went out for a few weeks, and I tried to hold out and not have sex, but we couldn't wait any longer. We started to hang out every day, and she was the sweetest, most generous girlfriend. She blew away every expectation I had of what a great relationship could be. She would come over every night, or I would go to her house. We would often fall asleep holding each other and did not want to leave one another. She was a good girl, though, and I would always take her home before her parents woke up. Except for one time when I dropped her off while her dad was leaving for the day. I was so embarrassed. He told me not to do that again. I didn't.

I spent many nights on the couch at her parents' house, and another morning, we woke up to her mom walking in the kitchen. We wanted to stay together all the time. One night, while saying goodbye, we just stood in her parents' kitchen and held each other for the longest time. Neither of us wanted to let go. We got that feeling that is unexplainable, almost breathless and tingling all over. I wrote, "I <3 U" on her heart. I wanted to be with her forever. No other woman compared to her. It was awesome, and a few months later, I planned to ask her to marry me on Valentine's Day.

Then we had our first fight a few days before I was going to ask her, and I thought maybe it was not meant to be. We made up quickly, and a week or two later, I asked her if she would marry me. She just looked at me and did not answer. I said, "Would you marry me?" Then, when she didn't answer right away, I said, "Someday... maybe?" and she replied, "Someday... maybe... if you ask me."

We just had one major hurdle to overcome. She wanted to keep her maiden name, but I disagreed, and we were at an impasse. After growing up in a dysfunctional home, I wanted a traditional family. This may seem piggish or stubborn, but it was important enough for me to not get married if she would not make this sacrifice. She was a strong-willed, independent woman and did not want to lose her identity, so I sent her a rose with a card that said, "A rose by any other name is still a rose." We debated for a month or so about the topic before we finally compromised on her using both last names.

Now that we had finally decided to get married, it was time to talk to her parents. When I shared our plans and asked her dad for his permission, I told him that we had been talking about getting married and asked him what he thought of the idea. He said, "Oh, crap." I didn't know what to think of his first reaction, but he then said he knew she was in love. She'd had boyfriends before, but he knew this was different. Before we left the house, her mom had reserved the church and the reception for six months later, on her birthday. After all, that would be a day I could not possibly forget!

During our dating and engagement, we spent every moment we could together. Leigh would come hang out with me at the men's bowling league. One of my friends in the league sat with us one night and told Leigh Ann that we took a vote and decided she was the best-looking woman in the bowling alley. Considering there was only the lady who worked there and the mom of one of the other guys, it was funny. He was a character, and we traded jokes all the time. He was pretty crazy, and if you weren't wearing a belt when he was around, your pants would end up around your ankles. It was really difficult to pull them up when you were standing there with a bowling ball in your hand. I remember when his first child was born. He had a son, and they announced it in the bowling alley.

I kept working hard and going to meetings, and once we were engaged, we started to look for a bigger place. I worked seven days a week. We planned the wedding and picked our bridesmaids and groomsmen. Uncle Buck was my best man, and the rest were friends from high school. We went to a strip club for my bachelor party, and I stayed sober while my friends all got wasted. Uncle Buck made sure we left before things got out of hand. Just before we got married, we put a deposit on a two-bedroom apartment. The place looked great and was in a nice neighborhood.

The night before we were married, we had our rehearsal dinner, and my bride-to-be gave me a set of golf clubs and a membership to the country club, which was within walking distance of our new apartment. I had driven by the country club for two years and thought it would be cool to belong to the club. It was surrounded by a large hedge row, and my rebellious side just wanted to be a member because I was such a hooligan.

Our wedding day arrived on my wife's birthday in 1992. We were young and in love, and the wedding was like a fairy tale. It was a perfect sunny day in September, not too hot or too cool. We were married in a beautiful church, and all of our friends and family were there. We left the church in a horse and carriage to go to the reception. It was a surprise for my new bride. As we left the church, kids from the neighborhood chased behind us, saying, "She looks like a princess!" They were right, and I was the luckiest man alive. Our honeymoon was fantastic, too, and everything went perfectly until we got home.

The nice little apartment we rented was ruined by popcorn paint on everything. The ceiling, the walls, trim, doors, inside closets, and even the door handles were sprayed. It was a mess and led to our second fight, but our first as a married couple. She was hysterical, and I was angry. My temper came back again, and I gently slapped her on the cheek and told her to get it together. She cried, and I felt terrible; she did not deserve that, and I thought our marriage was going to be over in the second week.

Although it seemed the honeymoon was over already, we reconciled. Her grace toward me was amazing. She deserved so much better, and I was a very selfish person. She blew away all of my expectations as a wife, yet I expected her to be perfect all the time. I did not handle it well when she was upset or angry with me. We did not fight often, but when we did, it would get ugly, and we both became physically, verbally, and emotionally abusive. In spite of our blow-ups, we always made up and were both too stubborn to give up. She would yell at me and tell me to leave, and I would yell back, "I am not leaving. You get out!" We were both so determined to not let the other one win the fight that we would stay, often in the same bed, just because we thought the other person should be on the couch! Our friends would say it was like the *War of the Roses*, that movie where the couple fell off the stairs while fighting and died in the foyer. While taking their last breath, the husband reaches out to touch his wife, and she pushes his hand away. I told her one time that the only way she would get out of this marriage was a murder-suicide. She replied, "Which one do I get to do?" I had met my match in every way.

We wanted to buy a house, so we started looking for a home and saved money for the down payment. We found a great little house not far from the country club. When we went to look at it, the agent gave us the key to go check it out. His secretary typed up the contract for us, and we did not meet the agent until settlement, when he picked up a commission check for over $3,000. I thought, *Man, we did all of the work, and he got a nice check; I could do that job!* We bought the house for $52,000 and fixed it up. I replaced the roof, and we remodeled the kitchen and built a white picket fence. I started playing golf every day and hanging out at the pool at the country club.

We had a great time playing house and started planning for a family. On our first anniversary, we planned a trip to France. This was where we did away with the birth control. When we returned from our trip, we found out that a baby boy was coming. I was so excited when we saw the sonogram. His balls were huge; there was no doubt it was a boy! I had a picture of the sonogram and showed all of my friends. I got a laugh every time I said, "Look at the big nuts on this little guy!"

I also decided to make a career change. I signed up for the real estate course. It was a ninety-day course, two nights a week. I sat in front of the class and paid attention and participated. I aced the class and passed the state exam on the first try. When I took the state exam, there were questions about having a criminal record, and I lied, saying I did not have a record. I became a real estate agent the same month my son was born, in May of 1994.

We did our best to watch him ourselves. My wife would work seven to three, and I would stay home with the little guy. I remember watching him hold his head up, begin to crawl, and start to understand what was going on around him. It was awesome, and I would just spend time holding him. Being a father was the greatest thing, and I just couldn't imagine walking out on him and my wife. My wife often complimented me on what a great father I was, as she had known I would be. I was a kid at heart and loved every part of fatherhood except for the dirty diapers. I took him with me everywhere: the real estate office, golf course, swimming pool, and bike rides. I would spend hours videotaping his every move. Nap time was my favorite. There was no better feeling in the world than holding my sleeping baby boy.

Selling real estate was fun for me. I loved meeting new people and helping them improve their lives. I worked other jobs to get by while I was getting established in the real estate business. I helped my wife's uncle build a house and do some masonry in his concrete business. I also sold promotional items such as pens and magnets.

Selling real estate is a roller coaster ride. Early in my career, there was a period where I made $300 in three months, but then everything I was working on settled, and I made $30,000 in thirty days. Once this happened, I knew we would make it. I came up with a slogan: "If you can find a phone, you can find Frank." First, I had a pager, then a cell phone, and I answered no matter the time or where I was.

One of the first people I met in real estate was a mortgage guy. He was about the same age as me and was just getting started in the mortgage business. He was hilarious and still reminds me of Chris Farley from *Saturday Night Live*. We hit it off instantly and began to hang out frequently, playing golf and doing business. I sent him all of my real estate clients to do mortgages. We both worked hard, and our business grew.

Meanwhile, at the golf course, I met a lot of people and started playing in the weekly golf league. There was a guy that grew up in Seaford and had a computer business. He ran network systems and needed some help running wire at night, so I helped him here and there. Starting out in real estate does not provide an immediate income, so the extra money was a help to us as well. He had a daughter born the same month as Zak. We hung out often, and he introduced me to many of his contacts. Two guys, in particular, became golfing buddies and friends for years. They were cousins and owned trucking companies. Both of these guys were very supportive of me and my growth in the real estate business. They introduced me to many of their employees, and they bought and sold many properties, which really helped my business.

As our success grew, Leigh and I bought a boat and started to go out on the river. I had a stick shift, and the first time I put in at the boat ramp, my parking brake slipped, and the truck started to slide into the water. I had stepped out of the truck to unload the boat when this happened, so a friend who was with me jumped in the truck and held the brake. The muffler was gurgling underwater, and my friend's leg was shaking as he floored it to pull the empty trailer out of the water. It was a close one, but we had a great time on the river. My wife grew up sailing, so she was nervous on a power boat. She always wanted to slow down.

We made a small profit from the sale of our first house and bought a bigger home in a nicer neighborhood still near the country club, and we were expecting our second child. We had the sonogram, and they could not tell us for sure if it was a boy or a girl. My wife was extra moody, so I knew it had to be a girl. I would tease her, saying only two women could be that moody. In her defense, I was hogging all the free time, and she was carrying the load at home and still working. I would tell her I had appointments and then go play golf with my friends. Often, she would find out and give me a hard time. I started to live by the motto that it is easier to get forgiveness than permission. She did not like this term or my tactics, but I continued to do what I wanted in spite of her resistance. I just dismissed her mood swings as hormones from being pregnant with a girl.

Leigh Ann's grandparents were in their eighties when we got married. They lived on a horse farm down the road from where Leigh Ann grew up on River Road. Like me, Leigh Ann's grandfather was born on the Fourth of July, and her grandmother was still riding horses at eighty-five. I helped them on the farm one day a week when we met, cutting grass, pulling weeds, and loading horse feed. They would always pay me well, and I was grateful. When we were looking for our second home, they offered to give us a lot in a really nice development they owned with a partner. All we had to do was pay their partner for the other half. We decided to buy the lot right after we bought the new house in 1995. We also purchased two duplexes with the plan to pay them off before our kids went to college so we could sell them or use the equity for their college fund.

When Leigh Ann was eight months pregnant, we were invited to my parents' for my dad's birthday dinner. That day, we got into an argument about fixing up the baby's room and how it was to be done. She decided that she was not going, so I went by myself. When I arrived, I saw a lot of cars that looked familiar, and when I got inside, all of our friends were there and asked where Leigh Ann was. My parents had planned a surprise baby shower for us. Talk about a surprise. I called Leigh Ann and explained the situation, and she finally came.

At last, our daughter was due. Our doctor had become a client, and I had sold some houses for him after our son was born. He had a plane, and he took me for a ride. Everything was going well while in the delivery room, and he asked if I wanted to deliver her. I asked him what I should do, and he said just gently pull her out and hold on tight because she would be slippery. It was awesome and love at first sight. She was beautiful and had a full head of hair. It was actually growing down her neck. Everywhere I took her, people commented on how gorgeous she was.

But her looks were deceiving. She had an awful time going to sleep and was inconsolable. She screamed so loud and often that we quit going out in public as much. It was an ear-piercing scream, like nails on a chalkboard.

One night, while trying to console her, I started to shake her a little, saying, "What is wrong with you?" My wife saw this and asked what was wrong with *me*. She could not console her either. With our son, we had a baby monitor, and he would sleep through the night and hardly make a sound. With our daughter, we turned off the baby monitor and stuffed towels under her door so we could try to get some sleep. We just had to let her cry herself to sleep. There was nothing we could do. She did this for months, and when she started walking, she would still scream every time she wanted something. It was tough for all of us. It even made our son angry, and he was only three. He would just say, "You don't share nice" when she would scream.

My wife started to attend church, but I was always looking for a reason not to go. I would have a tee time or a flag football game. I also started to skip out on my support group meetings. I became more concerned about pursuing the American Dream than serving God.

Blessings had started to come in so many ways. I quickly became a top producer in our local real estate market. We fixed up our home, and I had a lot of golfing buddies. Leigh Ann took the kids to the pool at the country club, and she was a great tennis player. We started playing in a tennis league, and life was good. We took vacations and traveled to Disney World, Las Vegas, and Hawaii. We purchased some rental properties and bought a bigger boat. We took the kids on boat trips. It seemed as though life was perfect.

But, no matter how good things were going, it was never good enough. I always wanted more in life. While I knew drugs and alcohol did not work for me, I became consumed with everything else the world could offer. I was never content. I wanted more money, newer golf clubs, a bigger house, more friends, and status. God was giving me everything I wanted in life, and privately, I thanked Him, but outwardly, I did not give Him any credit. Only a few people knew I believed in God. I told raunchy jokes, cursed like a sailor, and was addicted to sex and pornography. I felt like a hypocrite when I went to church and would show up late and sneak out early. I also quit going to meetings because I was more concerned with what people thought of me than helping others. I joined the local Lion's Club and began to do good deeds, hoping to make amends for my sins. As I began to gain success and status, I became concerned about who knew about my past. I still had shame and wanted to present a good image for the sake of my business.

I started playing a weekly poker game with many of our friends: my brother-in-law; Chad, the teacher; Chef Boy, the mechanic; Thunder, the banker; the mortgage man; The Man, manufacturer/importer; River, the guidance counselor; the used car dealer/appraiser; Bundy, the shoe salesman; Fish, the school tech guru; the factory manager; the three police officers; the Junk man; the insurance salesman; the restaurant supply salesman; and Meat Man, the food distributor, were just some of the crew. First, we started playing at my house, then The Man's, and eventually, we ended up in River's basement. We called it the dungeon because it was filled with smoke and a bunch of misfits. It was always fun and never for a lot of money. We would talk about everything from our wives and kids to politics to religion, and we were a pretty diverse group in our beliefs. Republicans, Democrats, conservatives, liberals, believers, non-believers, Protestants, Catholics, and atheists. Most of us were middle-aged, middle-class, married white guys and had pretty good jobs and families. There were some divorces and other struggles, but for the most part, it was a solid group of men.

As the years went on, the dungeon crew grew. Some of the men's kids got old enough to play, and they started to bring their friends over. River was the host with the most and would always allow anyone to come over. He played vinyl records and smoked cigars and was just an all-around great guy. It was typical to have thirty or more guys playing cards in the dungeon every Friday night. We would curse, tell stories, play cards, and laugh till all hours. Often, I would drive people home, as many of the guys would drink and smoke too much. Throughout the night, there were things that we would say—usually imitating the mortgage man, who was always the funniest. When the game or the conversation got too serious, and someone would start whining or complaining, we would count one, two, three and then cry, "Wahhhhhhhhh!" It would always get a laugh and lighten the situation. Also, anytime someone would ask, "Can I raise?" he would reply, "You can do all things through Christ who strengthens you [Philippians 4:13]." Whenever he would do something, he would say, "I said to myself, 'Self, why did you do that?'"

I stayed sober, and the guys would often ask why I did not drink. I told them I was allergic to alcohol. When I drank, I broke out in handcuffs. Some people could do things in moderation, and I was not one of them. Everything I did was all or nothing.

My wife can sing like an angel and was asked to do special music at church one day. She practiced and practiced, singing "El Shaddai." I remember how well she did and was not surprised when she was asked to join the praise team. She had finally found her calling. She would go to practice once or twice a week and then church on Sundays. She would always ask me to come, but I would make excuses or tell her I would be there and just sleep in. She had to go early to practice, so I would bring the kids later. Sometimes, I would take the kids to the nursery at church, sit in the back pew for a little while, then leave to play golf or flag football.

To me, life seemed to be going great, but my wife was not very happy with our marriage, and we fought more and more. She was still playing tennis and singing at church, and I couldn't wait for her to go. No matter how miserable we were, she would always come home from church singing and in a good mood. Sunday mornings were great, but the rest of the week got tougher and tougher. It was like we were having a power struggle. Both of us wanted to be in control, and neither one wanted to lose.

In 1997, we had been married for five years. Zak was three, and Hailey was one. That was when we got some bad news. My uncle Buck was diagnosed with colon cancer. He began a long battle with treatments and surgeries. He never complained and kept working the whole time. His family had moved a couple of hours away because my aunt was going to pharmacy school, so we did not see each other as much.

When the kids were about four and two, my sister met this guy who put on a good act. He pretended to care about her. They got engaged, and she became pregnant. Right before the wedding, she found out he was living a lie and was hooked on crack. My sister had no idea, and he took no responsibility. My business was growing, I needed the help, and she had her real estate license, so I hired her as an assistant, and she moved in with us. Her little boy was born on the same day as my son, four years later. She helped watch the kids, worked at the office, and talked to my wife. Women use three times the words men do, so I would come home from work and be ready for chill time, and Leigh Ann would want to talk. When Angel moved in, I didn't have to talk as much!

Angel really helped our business and with the kids. I was able to work any time, and my income went from $30,000 in my first full year to $60,000 in my second and $120,000 in my third. By my fourth year, I was making over $200,000. It seemed like everyone I spoke to wanted to buy or sell a home. As much as I liked making a lot of money, it did not control my motives.

Another motto I used was that it is more important to make a friend than to make a sale. One example of this was during my second year in the business when there was a client who wanted to purchase a lot in a nice community. When I presented the offer to the developer, he informed me that he would not pay me a commission because my broker was suing him for a commission on another deal. When I asked my broker what I should do, he instructed me to tell my client that the lot was not available and sell them something else. This did not sit right with me, so I referred them directly to the developer. I told them the situation and advised them to buy the lot they wanted without my involvement. The commission would have been great, but it did not matter in the big picture. They took me and my wife to dinner and have referred millions of dollars in sales since then. This client had a small business at the time, which grew to a hundred-million-dollar company, and he still sends a lot of business our way.

Another good friend I met when I first started was a realtor and also an auctioneer. He had recently sold his video business and gotten into real estate. He was pretty tech-savvy, and between him and my tech friend, I was on the cutting edge of real estate, with a bag phone, pager, a digital camera, and a laptop. There were no other agents who were using technology like this in our market.

I changed brokerage firms in '96, and my business continued to grow. One day, while on the sales tour, we rode through a new development. There were "for sale by owner" signs, and being the only agent with a cell phone, I called the developer before we got back to the office. I found out the lots were not selling because the developer wanted 30 percent over the current market value. I had sold a home in another development where I met a builder. I recommended the developer partner with the builder to sell lot and home packages so the lot price would be rolled into the package and the developer could get top dollar. The builder had inventory and a great product, and I had lots and home packages to sell, which meant higher commissions. The buyers were happy because they got a great product and bought it just before the market was about to explode. This builder became a good friend and golfing buddy. He and his partner had three other developments, and I introduced them to one more, giving me five developments to sell out.

As I approached thirty years old, everything was going great. I became the top producer in our market and was nationally recognized by *REALTOR Magazine* as one of the thirty under thirty. This was a big deal for me, as my whole life, I considered myself just average. I had never received any notable recognition in my life. The only trophy I ever received was for soccer, second-team all-conference, in my junior year of high school. It was in the All-Catholic Conference, which consisted of only four schools in our state. My wife, on the other hand, grew up riding horses and had probably won a hundred competitions. She had a room full of trophies. She hardly ever lost and set a very high standard for everything. That now included me. I was a born slacker, and she would not let me just slide by, no matter how hard I tried.

We set these expectations for our children as well. At an early age, we instilled independence in them. When the kids started school, we had them set their alarm to get themselves up and ready. Leigh was a great mother. When the kids went to school, we followed the school bus while she cried and took pictures of them getting on and off the bus. Every day the kids came home, she had homemade cookies waiting for them. It was great; she was doing all of the work, and I would play with the kids. I thought life was perfect, but she did not. I was working and playing golf and playing with the kids while she felt trapped and was not having any fun. We began to argue more and more.

The kids started to play sports, and I started coaching. I loved it, but I was often very hard on them. They played T-ball and did very well. At two years old, Zak had incredible hand-eye coordination. Before he could walk, he had an Exersaucer, and we would put a golf ball in the tray. He would spin around chasing the ball until he made himself dizzy. It was hilarious to watch. When he got a hold of the golf ball, he would throw it, and you'd better be paying attention! With a plastic bat, he could throw a ball in the air and hit it every time. He would just go out in the yard and play all day. We were playing catch when he was three.

Coaching was a blast since I was still a big kid at heart. I was able to play with my kids, meet tons of clients, and just have fun. Leigh Ann, being the psych major she was, told me we should let the kids win until they were six-year-olds to build their confidence. Once they turned six, we should not let them win anymore. So, we made them earn it. I built a wall in the backyard for Zak to kick a ball against, and he would spend hours kicking with both feet. I showed him how to pick a spot and hit it. Whatever he was doing, he would work at it until he became an expert.

Zak was always smaller and quieter than the other kids, but he would always impress people with his determination and abilities. He was extremely shy and did not like to talk to other people very much. When he was about nine years old, on Little League picture day, he did not want to get his picture taken. He fought with me about going, and I spanked him. The whole family was a mess, but he did what I made him do and even grimaced for the picture. Then game time came, and we were playing the Giants. Zak and his best friend Nick were two of the littlest guys in the league and played for the Orioles. The Giants were appropriately named, and the team was stacked with all of the biggest and best players in the league. It was literally a David versus Goliath match-up. No one thought we had a chance, but our kids kept hanging around, getting walked, and stealing bases. The Giant pitchers were throwing so hard that our players couldn't get the bat turned around fast enough. The game came down to the final inning, and we were down by three runs. We told our players to start taking pitches, and they walked the bases loaded. Our players were so little that they couldn't get in the strike zone. Zak came up to bat with two outs, and we told him to take pitches until he got a strike because we hadn't hit the ball all day or scored a run. He swung at the first pitch and tipped the ball. I was livid that he wasn't going to listen to me. He swung at the second pitch also and had two strikes. Then, on the third pitch, he hit a line drive down the first base line. I was coaching third and told him to hold up at second, but he ran to third anyway. He cleared the bases and slid in safe.

The score was now tied, and he was the winning run on third. After two strikes on the next batter, Zak stole home, and the tag was there in plenty of time. I was trying to hold him back at third, but he went anyway. As he slid into the home, the ball came out of the glove, and we won the game. Everyone went wild, and the head coach picked him up on his shoulders and carried him off the field. If you looked at the lineup, you would never think we could have won that game. He was shy about many things, but he was fearless in so many others. He never stopped impressing me, defiantly beating the odds and his opponents. He was on every all-star team and won more than one championship in Little League, yet he always listened to the other coaches more than me. Eventually, when I saw him doing something that needed to be corrected, I just started telling the other coach what to tell him, and he would do it with no rebellion.

Ultimately, we signed the kids up for everything: soccer, Little League, swim team. They also learned to golf and play tennis. Leigh was an excellent tennis player, and the kids became quite good as well. We wanted them to learn as much as possible, and we did not let them quit anything until they became good at whatever sport they were playing. Of course, once they became good at it, they did not want to quit. Hailey also played field hockey and cheerleading, and they both went to gymnastics for a little while.

Leigh Ann would make sure the kids had everything they needed, and of course, they did not always appreciate what she did, and neither did I. Don't get me wrong, most days were like a dream come true, but when the wife wasn't happy, no one was happy. Our marriage seemed perfect to me, but Leigh was tired of doing all of the heavy lifting. I kept denying there was a problem and tried to minimize her complaints.

My friend from the bowling alley had a daughter as well, and she was a year older than Hailey. As they grew up, our kids began to play together. They always had a good time, and we even went on family vacations together. They owned a music store, and his wife became a good friend as well. They always had a Christmas party where Santa Claus would come. The kids loved it, and we were the biggest kids of all. He was always playing pranks and spoiling the kids.

One day, while we were playing golf, he kept riding in front of us, so we yelled, "Fore," like a ball was coming at him. He dove on the ground and got grass stains on the knees of his brand-new khaki pants. My builder friend and I laughed and laughed. About a month later, he told me he had free passes to play a course about forty minutes from our hometown. It was during the week, and I had a busy day at work. He kept calling to see where I was. When I was about five minutes from the course, he called and said, "Fooore." There were no passes to play golf. He was getting even for the grass stains on his pants.

The next week, at a Lion's Club Crab Feast, he tapped my elbow while I was drinking a Sprite, and I spilled some on myself. When I tried to tap his elbow while he was drinking a beer, he threw the whole beer on the guy next to him and made it look like it was my fault. I was embarrassed and mad, so I went outside and let the air out of all four of his tires. He didn't speak to me for six months. While motocross trail riding, he crashed and was not wearing his helmet. He was in a coma for ten days. I went to visit him often, and when he finally came to, my mortgage friend and I went to see him. He had nearly died and was just coming out of the fog. My friend gave him a high five, and when I tried to do the same, he pulled his hand away. He was still mad at me. We both laughed; we were just glad that our buddy was going to live. He eventually forgave me, as I kept coming to see him and encouraged him while he learned to walk and talk again. Things were different after the accident.

For Zak's sixth birthday, I wanted to give him a basketball court, which meant a paved driveway and a net. Leigh and I had been arguing more than usual, and she was determined that I should not be tearing up the driveway before the birthday party. She took the key to the backhoe I had borrowed to tear out the old driveway and would not give it back, so I took the keys to her minivan. We had a stand-off, and neither of us would give in. Leigh called the cops on me. The police came to the house for a domestic disturbance. We were both so stubborn that it took a police officer to convince us both to give the keys back to one another.

Meanwhile, my sister and the kids were watching us act like spoiled children. It was embarrassing, but we were both too prideful to let the other one win. With the keys exchanged, she left, and I repaired the driveway.

Shortly after this conflict, we were arguing again, this time over something I don't even remember. I had made myself a sandwich, and she slapped the plate out of my hand, so I slapped her. My temper got the best of me, as it often did. I had no patience, and the negativity was tiresome. We did not get physical very often, but there were times when we wanted to kill each other. It got uglier and uglier. I felt terrible, and our marriage was falling apart. I called an attorney friend and told him I thought we should get a divorce. He knew Leigh Ann and told me I could not afford it and that I would never do any better. He was right.

Even though I was not attending church very often, I went to see our pastor. I was broken and did not know what else to do. He listened and advised that we go to a Christian counselor. Leigh Ann agreed to go. Many things came out during our counseling sessions. Leigh was convinced that I did not love her and that I only paid attention to her when I wanted sex. I felt like nothing I did was good enough for her. It was true that I did not help much around the house, but I was providing for my family. I was home every night and loved her deeply. She thought I just wanted sex, while I thought that is how you showed your wife you loved her. Actually, she just wanted me to help vacuum and do some dishes!

Finally, after several counseling sessions, she understood that I loved her and was not going anywhere. I really did love her, and I was sick to my stomach when I thought about us getting a divorce. Things got better, and our knockdown drag-out fights became few and far between. I would love to say they were gone forever, but they still popped up every once in a while. I think the fact that we could be completely hateful toward one another and then forgive each other showed how committed we were to sticking it out through thick and thin. Often, our fights would end in a stalemate. She would tell me to get out, and I would tell her to get out, but we were both too stubborn to leave, so we would make up eventually, and our love grew deeper. I knew there was no one else who would put up with me, and she was loyal and forgiving beyond what I deserved.

Now, most of our days were peaceful, and we were living out the American Dream—taking the kids to Disney World, going on boat trips in the summer, and ski trips in the winter months. We were dedicated to our children and very active parents. My sister, Angel, was getting her life together and moved out on her own. Shortly after she moved out, she met a guy and got pregnant. He married her, and they moved to his family farm, an hour away from where we lived. We missed her, but we hired a new assistant and then another one. Leigh Ann quit her job at the hospital and came to work with me while the kids were in school.

Usually, for Leigh Ann's birthday and our anniversary, we would take a trip with just the two of us. We traveled a lot in our first six years of marriage. After the trip to England and France, we went to the Grand Canyon, Las Vegas, and Aruba. In 1999, Leigh Ann was going to turn thirty years old, so for her thirtieth birthday, I planned to take her to Hawaii. She was not looking forward to turning thirty. She was almost depressed about it, like she was all of a sudden going to be old. I think some of her worries came from her insecurities in our marriage, the kids starting school, and her struggles with her job. In Hawaii, we had a great time and went sailing with an old high school friend who was living there. I went surfing on Waikiki, and we went snorkeling in Waimea Bay and hiking to the top of Diamond Head. She did shed a few tears about turning thirty, but she was just as beautiful as the day we met.

Even though I did not drink, most of my friends did, except for Chuck. He was sober for some time without going to meetings because he had many DUIs at an early age. We had a lot in common and hit it off immediately. I was going to meetings less and less and was living vicariously through my friends. Most of my friends were guys from the country club, coaching, and friends of our kids. Some drank a little, but many drank a lot. We had just started hanging out. For my thirtieth birthday, we had a big party at our house. We had a moon bounce for the kids and a keg for the adults. Just because I was an alcoholic and addict did not mean everyone was, so I would buy drinks for my friends. He started drinking again at my birthday party. I did not think much about it, and it did not seem like a big problem at first.

It was about this time that I started planning golf trips with my buddies. Sixteen of us went to Myrtle Beach for a long weekend. I was the designated driver and stayed sober the whole time, but I lived vicariously through my friends as everyone drank all the way there. On one of the trips, I was driving Chuck's 560 Mercedes. This thing was built for the autobahn. We were cruising along at eighty miles per hour, and it felt like fifty, so we decided to see what it would do. I sped up to one hundred, then one hundred and ten, one hundred and twenty, one hundred and thirty, when one of my buddies said, "You should go one hundred and forty just to say you did it!" We hit one hundred and forty and then some traffic, so we finally slowed down—it was a miracle that we did not get thrown in jail or wreck. Halfway there, the guys passed out, and I would slam on the brakes and scream to mess with them. It was funny until the seventh time when my buddy Chuck punched me a dozen times while I was driving.

The first golf course we went to had a strip club owners' convention playing on the same course. There were strippers everywhere, and they were giving out drinks and lap dances. At the time, we thought how lucky we were until word got back to some of the wives. Then it wasn't so cool. One of my buddies came home to his clothes out on the front lawn. My wife was a little bit more understanding but still hurt. I justified our actions, saying it was just guys having fun. Actually, it was torture because it was just a tease. One of the guys took some pictures, and I stole the camera, took the film, and destroyed the evidence. One of the girls was so drunk she fell off a moving golf cart while naked. Once again, it was fun until it wasn't. It seemed like everything went too far without ever feeling fulfilled.

I was making a ton of money and spent every dime. Leigh and I still had fights, mostly about money and disciplining the kids. She was upset because I was having all the fun, and she was doing all the work. I didn't see the problem. I told her she could do whatever she wanted and to just let me know what she wanted to do. She started playing in a weekly tennis league, and this helped. I was working, playing golf three times a week, going to Lion's Club on Mondays, playing poker on Fridays, and flag football on Sundays. Saturdays were reserved for family time, Little League, soccer, or going out on the boat.

CHAPTER 10:

Frank's Island

Another one of my best friends is my brother-in-law, who is married to Leigh's sister. When we first met, he was a videographer who filmed a home show doing tours of houses and properties that aired on local TV on Sunday mornings, while my sister-in-law was a TV anchorwoman. They had kids who were about the same age as ours, so the cousins were together all the time, and my brother-in-law and I would play golf and poker regularly. He became the brother I always wanted, and we have had a ton of fun over the years.

On his birthday, October 10, 2000, he called me up and asked if we would like to buy an island. He had just filmed the property and was really excited. It was twenty acres of heaven on the Chesapeake Bay with a beautiful beach, a bungalow, dunes, trees, and trails. I saw the pictures and thought it was a million-dollar property. The owner was only asking $156,000. I thought it must be washing away.

We set up a tour for a few days later on Friday the 13th. I thought this was a good sign, considering it was the anniversary of my salvation. When we turned right on Roland Parks Rd., I thought that was another good sign, considering my last name is Parks. At the end of the road was another sign that said Lee Avenue. It was spelled differently, but the signs were piling up. This island is located in Chance, MD, and I thought,

What are the chances? We had been looking for a waterfront property, and we had finally found one.

My wife and sister-in-law wanted to name the island after their family name, and my brother-in-law wanted to call it Birthday Island because he found it on his birthday. I knew I was outvoted, so I simply asked the owner, "What is the name of this island?" He replied, "It has always been called Frank's Island." Immediately, they asked about changing the name, but the owner said they had already tried, and it was not possible because it had been recorded in deeds and on maps. Of course, I thought the name was perfect!

Regardless of the name, we were sold. I recommended we pay full price, as the owner was willing to finance the property for us, and still felt like I had won the lottery. We settled on November 2, 2000, and spent our first night on the island right after closing. It was dark when we got there, and I could not wait until morning to see the sunrise. I was absolutely amazed by the beauty of God's creation. When we arrived, it was like the cares of the world were left behind. There was amazing wildlife: deer, foxes, and ducks. It was so peaceful, and we so greatly enjoyed our time away as a family. There was no cell service or cable, so we spent time exploring, playing games, and building sandcastles. I just felt closer to my family and God on the island than ever before. We did not want to leave at the end of that first weekend, but we had to go back to reality.

Thankfully, the island was only an hour from home, and we would go as often as possible, spending weekends and time when the kids were off from school. Leigh would always leave early Sunday morning to go back to Seaford for church. Even in cold weather, she would paddle across the creek and drive an hour to worship and sing for God. Often, I tried to convince her to stay on the island and just quit the praise band, but she would always reply that our life was so blessed because of her favor and faithfulness to God. I couldn't argue, but I kept trying to do the devil's work and convince her that she should just spend time with us. My motives were completely selfish, and she was not fooled.

From the time I started in real estate, I wanted to open my own brokerage. After becoming the top producer, I approached my broker about becoming a partner. He was always very supportive of my career and success but did not want a partner. I had an assistant who was getting her license and said that if I opened my own company, she would be my first agent. I started writing my listing agreements to allow a seller to cancel with five days' notice and gave all of my clients an option to leave or stay—95 percent of them came with me, so we started our new business.

When we opened in 2002, I thought if we could get five agents in five years and make at least five sales a month, we could make a living. Within three years, we had thirty agents and were closing thirty sales per month. The boom had begun, and I thought it would never quit. Many of my clients and friends became agents, and ten or more of them were making over 100,000 per year. During our first full year in business, we grossed over one million dollars in commissions. We also started to manage rental properties. One of our agents was a former client, and he decided to specialize in property management. Needless to say, we were living high on the hog. I had thousands of dollars to spend every week and did just that. Making money became addicting, and spending money became a rush. We bought jet skis for the island, boats, kayaks, and all kinds of water toys. Leigh Ann bought me a 1967 Mustang convertible for our tenth anniversary.

Money masked our problems for a while, but I still did not deserve her. She made sure the kids and I had everything we wanted. I was so spoiled it was ridiculous. Everything I wanted came to me, yet I just kept trying to get more.

We spent nine years in the house on Willey Street, and most of the time we were there, I was looking for our dream home on the river. In 2003, we finally bought a lot on the Nanticoke in the same development where we bought the lot from Leigh Ann's grandparents. This lot had been attached to a house that I had sold previously. We worked out a deal with the seller and Chuck to buy the house with no commission if we could buy the lot for a discounted price. It was Chuck's dream to live on the river as well. He had started doing appraisals and was also doing quite well, so we would be neighbors. Although I was really excited and wanted to build right away, Leigh Ann did not want the kids to change schools and was not ready, so we waited.

In the summer of 2002, Uncle Buck, Aunt Kay, Jason, and Lindsay came to the island to visit. We rode jet skis and splashed each other and had a blast. It seemed like Uncle Buck was winning his battle with cancer. In 2003, he came back, and we just went fishing. We spent the day pulling in perch and had a great time. He spent the night, and the next day, he was pretty sick. He was feeling so bad I had to help him get in the car when Aunt Kay had to take him home. The cancer was starting to catch up with him.

In February 2004, Uncle Buck was losing his battle. Leigh Ann and I went to visit him a few days before he passed. He was in and out of consciousness. He had lost a lot of weight and was basically skin and bones. When he would go out of consciousness, he would reach into the air and move his hands as if he were still turning wrenches. We knew his time with us was coming to an end. A few days later, Aunt Kay called and told us he was gone, and they would wait for us to come see him before they took him away. We left right away. When we got there, we knelt beside him, cried, and prayed for God to take him into heaven.

I never knew where Uncle Buck stood with God, but I knew he was a good man. I had never experienced the death of a loved one so close or so young. He was only forty-seven, and it hit close to home. I started to seek God more and wonder if our prayers were heard and if he was in heaven. I did not get the answer right away, but several months after Uncle Buck died, I saw him in a dream. He looked perfect, like an angel. He was glowing and did not say a word. He just winked at me to let me know he was okay. I was relieved to know he was at peace.

Our outlook on life changed when Uncle Buck passed. A long life is not promised, especially on my side of the family. Shortly after Uncle Buck died, Leigh Ann agreed to start building our dream home on the river. Business was nearing two million in gross commissions, and we could afford to do it, so she gave in. We spent the next month or so working on our plans. We customized some drawings for a modern Victorian with a wraparound porch, four fireplaces, a custom kitchen, an oversized garage, and a full basement for a man cave and poker room. We would also have a pier and dock for our new boat and jet skis. My builder buddies gave us a deal on the house, and we started construction in May of 2004.

Chuck was already living next door and loving it. We went in on a pair of brand-new jet skis. He bought a blue one, and I bought a red one. We would take the kids tubing on the boat and jet skiing. While we were building the house, I would get the kids to help. They would be bugging me to go tubing, and I would tell them the faster I got done, the faster we could go tubing. Chuck's son, Aaron, was about six years old and would come over every day to see what we were doing. He would ask if he could drive the bobcat, go up in the boom lift, and use the nail gun. Whatever we were working on, he would be right there helping. He was riding motocross, and Chuck started riding, as well. Aaron was winning a room full of trophies, while Chuck won a new nickname: "Crash."

While the house was under construction, I was able to work there every day. Business was going well, and my bowling buddy Phil was an electrician. He and I wired the entire house. Every week, I would go to work on Wednesday for the company sales meeting and tour, get a big check from all of the closings and property management, work on the house till all hours, take the kids on the boat, and get them to their sports practices the rest of the week. Many of the parents of kids I coached bought houses. I would talk to clients on the cell phone while coaching soccer or baseball. Often, I was there in body, but my mind was elsewhere. I loved playing with the kids and tried to be engaged, but there were times when I was checked out and the assistant coaches took over. I actually preferred the role of assistant coach because I could have more flexibility. I helped Phil with our daughter's T-ball team while I was coaching Zak in baseball and both kids in soccer as well. He gave me a team hat with "Coach No Show" embroidered on the back.

I was spreading myself thin in many areas, and eventually, my business would suffer because I was spending more time on the house and with my family than I was working. It was during this same time that Phil's wife was diagnosed with breast cancer. She had surgery and came through okay, but she was not the same. She was really angry with life and Phil especially. Their marriage started to fall apart, and my wife and I tried to counsel them, but it kept going the wrong way. Phil and I worked on the house every day together, and he kept disappearing. His wife confronted me about how much he was getting paid and where his money was going. I was paying him, but he was beginning to struggle with pain pills. They separated, and the marriage ended. Breast cancer took his wife, and he lost his daughter in a car accident. His addiction took over for a while, but he eventually got off the pills and remarried. His life is good today.

In January 2005, we moved into our dream home, and I started planning our next project: building a new office for our team. We had outgrown the 1,000-square-foot office and doubled our space to 2,000 square feet, but we still needed more. We bought a couple of acres of property down the road from our existing office and drew plans for 8,500 square feet., of which we would occupy 4,000 square feet and sell the other 4,500 square feet as office condos to help pay for the $1.2 million project. We coordinated the project to start in 2006 to be done in 2007 when our current lease was ending.

Since 1994, my real estate career had increased every year, and I thought that it was going to last forever. Our company was bringing in over two million dollars in commissions, and I was spending as fast as it was coming in.

We spent hundreds of thousands on extras for our house. We spent more on the cabinets and appliances than we did on our entire first house. The pier, dock, jet skis and water trampoline were over $50,000. We built a forty-by-sixty barn to store all of the toys. Our daughter wanted a pony, so we bought some land and built a barn down the road. We spent over $100,000 cash on the land and building. One day, I asked Chuck to go shopping with me to buy birthday presents for the kids. We bought a ping pong table for the man cave, a dirt bike for Zak, a four-wheeler for Hailey, and an orange scooter for Leigh Ann.

As my thirty-fifth birthday was approaching, I handed out about five hundred invitations to a party at the house, and over three hundred people came. There were so many people I did not get to speak to everyone. We had a band, an open bar, and an all-you-can-eat. Leigh Ann bought me a new four-wheeler for my birthday so I could go riding with the kids. I was living the high life and playing the Beastie Boys again. We rocked out to the song "You Gotta Fight for Your Right to Party!" I was sober, but not many other people were. I had friends take kids tubing and hired lifeguards, bartenders, a grill master, and servers. Chef Boy and Brother-in-Law hooked up an awesome spread with shrimp, bacon-wrapped scallops, and all kinds of desserts, along with the usual hamburgers and hot dogs. We had a fireworks show that rivaled those of nearby towns. By the end of the night, there were quite a few people stumbling around, and many people said it was the best party ever. We spent about $4,000 on the party and couldn't wait to do it again next year.

In 2005, our business brought in $2.2 million in commissions, and we gave out over $30,000 in bonus money to our agents and staff. I took home over $500,000 in income before taxes.

Leigh Ann always tried to control my spending, but she did not know exactly how much we were making or how much money I was spending until tax time. She would always help do taxes and say, "If we made that much money, where is it all?" I would carry around a thousand dollars at all times. I would always take my friends out to eat, drink, and play golf. We had a lot of money in the bank, and I could buy whatever I wanted. I bought four jet skis and all kinds of water toys. No matter what I bought, there was always another toy I wanted. We could go out the back door of our home, get on the boat, and go to our own private island. I was blessed to take off work whenever I wanted.

Then 2006 came, and the trials began. Leigh Ann had been complaining of headaches and was having toothaches that she was keeping secret. She was afraid of the dentist and had not gone in many years. I was on a weekend duck hunting trip on the island with some friends when Leigh Ann's headache became something much worse. Our neighbors called and told me that she was being picked up by an ambulance. When I arrived at the hospital, she had a one-hundred-and-four-degree temperature. They suspected that she had meningitis, but they did not know if it was bacterial or viral. Either one could be fatal, and the doctors were not taking any chances. They came to examine her in full outbreak gear with face shields and gloves. They told me that she could be very contagious. She needed help to move around, and I stayed with her every moment. We had friends come to the house to stay with the kids.

I began to pray and question God. She was the faithful one, always going to church and singing in the praise band. I was the one who deserved to be in the hospital bed, in pain, near death.

It was a Sunday afternoon. She had missed church for the first time in months, and her condition was not improving. We were still waiting for the diagnosis and decided to pray together. We both believed in God and had prayed individually throughout our marriage, but for the first time ever, we prayed together. We held hands and pleaded with God to help her get through this sickness. As soon as we said amen, our pastor arrived at the door with flowers, and at that moment, I knew she was going to be okay. He came in with no fear of contamination. I explained that she may have viral meningitis, and he just acted like there was no chance he could be infected.

His demeanor was the complete opposite of the doctors. They were fearing the worst-case scenario and speaking doom and gloom while he came in with the confidence of Christ.

He prayed with us again, and I left the room to go watch the Steelers' game with Leigh Ann's dad in the waiting room. He was having a really hard time with her being so sick, particularly since he'd had to bury Leigh Ann's older sister when she was ten years old. She had been ill often but suddenly died from Goodpasture syndrome. If she had not passed away, I am not sure they would have had any more children, but after her passing, they decided to have another child, and Leigh Ann was born. I started to realize that out of tragedy, God can make good.

It was the first round of the playoffs, and the Steelers had barely made it in as the sixth seed. They were playing the Bengals, and I remember early in the game, Carson Palmer went down with a knee injury. During the game, I kept checking on Leigh Ann. She did not want any lights on in the room or any noise. Her head was throbbing, and she could hardly move. I had to help her do everything. The doctors finally came and told us she had bacterial meningitis, and while she was not contagious, she still had a very fatal disease. The meningitis likely came from a tooth infection. The Steelers won and she was feeling a little better. I had been at the hospital for two days by this point, and she told me to go home and spend the night with the kids, so I did. I got a call late that night that her fever was spiking over one hundred and four, and they had moved her to the ICU. For the next week and a half, I went back to the hospital and only went home to shower and change clothes.

All in all, Leigh was in the hospital for eleven days on IV antibiotics. She finally got well enough to go home but still struggled with headaches and light sensitivity. While she recuperated, we watched the playoffs together as the Steelers kept winning and eventually beat the Broncos to earn a spot in Super Bowl 50. As soon as they won the game, Leigh Ann said I should go. I had been cheering for the Steelers to win their fifth ring, "one for the thumb," since I was a kid. She had seen how few chances they had and jokingly said, "You may not get to go to another one." She also commented how good I had been to stay by her side through her illness and that I deserved to go. I wasn't going to argue!

Zak was eleven and always by my side watching the games, and I was excited to take him with me. We flew to Detroit to watch the Steelers beat the Seattle Seahawks to finally get the one for the thumb. The game was awesome. I screamed so loud I nearly passed out. The Seattle fan next to me said, "This guy is killing me!" That night, when we went to bed, Zak said it was the coolest thing he had ever done. I replied, "Well, you're only eleven, just wait!"

We stayed in Windsor, Canada, just across the bridge from Detroit. It was amazing to me to see rows and rows of homes deserted. We toured the Ford Truck Plant and the Henry Ford Museum. You could see the city had once flourished with factories and workers; now, automation and exporting jobs to Mexico and China had decimated the city. Similarly, our hometown of Seaford was feeling the effects of the DuPont Nylon Factory leaving town.

I came home from the Super Bowl just as the real estate market started to decline. We had made and spent so much money in 2005 that we had a $60,000 tax bill. Suddenly, our savings were gone, and we started to borrow money to keep up with all the debt I had incurred. I kept up a good front on the outside, but I started to slip into a depression.

I became angry with my wife and children more easily, sometimes to the point of rage, and was both verbally and physically abusive. My marriage was struggling because my wife felt like I was only using her since I did very little to encourage or support her except pester her for sex. When she would turn me down, I escaped reality with a pornography addiction. I was also spending two nights a week playing cards with my friends and began losing money I couldn't afford to lose.

Suicidal thoughts began creeping in once more, and I felt like a fraud because I was. I did the best I could to make everything look great on the outside, but I was broken mentally and spiritually. I was having a hard time getting out of bed in the morning and was not sleeping well.

Eventually, I told my wife about the thoughts of suicide, and she did everything she could do to build me up and encourage me. I did not deserve the love and grace she gave to me, but she just kept forgiving me again and again. My kids did, as well. I was very hard on them as I coached them in every sport. Even if I weren't the coach, I would critique their play, attitude, and effort. I was constantly demanding perfection from them while living with my own demons.

Don't get me wrong, the bad times were pretty rough, but there were a lot of good times, as well. We were all still playing on the river, riding dirt bikes and four-wheelers, and playing paintball and all kinds of sports with all the kids in the neighborhood.

All the kids from the neighborhood, soccer, and school hung out. Our house was always full of kids, so I did my best to stay home and take them tubing and jet skiing. They loved it, and so did I. There were days when I had grass to cut and weeds to pull, and the kids would come over to help so they could go tubing sooner.

One day, we were taking the kids tubing when a little one of the kids wouldn't get on the boat. Chuck said, "Are you coming?"

He said, "I am waiting for adult supervision."

Chuck and I looked at each other and said, "We are adults, come on." He then informed us that his mom said Mr. Frank and Mr. Chuck are not considered adult supervision, so he stayed on the dock.

In his defense, he was recovering from a wipeout while hover tubing. If you have never been, I do not recommend trying this at home. If you put an eighty-pound kid on a tube behind a jet ski going fifty miles per hour, they will get airborne; if they are only seventy pounds, they aren't heavy enough to put it back down. After he went skipping across the water, we decided maybe hover tubing wasn't such a good idea.

Suffice it to say, it was truly a blast… and a miracle the kids survived.

It was around this time that Leigh Ann told me about a weekend church retreat that she wanted us to attend. She had asked me before, but I had quickly dismissed the idea. This time, she was adamant, and I could not say no. She had nearly died and let me go to the Super Bowl. I was not getting out of it this time, and we made plans to go in the fall.

The fun continued in the spring and summer of 2006. We began construction on the office building, borrowing over a million dollars as our five-year lease was running out at our current location, and we had outgrown the space. We planned to sell the building in four units to pay back a big part of the loan and then build another building on the lot next door to pay off the balance. I felt as though everything was going well with the business, and once the building was done, we would have a great place for all of our agents to work. We broke ground in the fall, and then I went on the retreat.

CHAPTER 11:

Surrender

I really thought I was going on this retreat to please my wife, but God had other plans. There were several speakers over the weekend, and every talk moved me closer to a relationship with Jesus. I had been walking the fence for too long. I was thirty-six years old and had pursued everything in life but Jesus to find fulfillment. I tried drugs and alcohol, pornography, sex, money, status, work, success, family, fatherhood, and charity work, yet it all fell short of contentment. After the weekend, everything was different, but I still had issues and a lot of sins to reconcile.

I began praying all the time. Instead of talking to myself, I started talking to God and asking Him what I should do every day. One of the first things I did when I got home was give away my porn collection. (Coincidentally, the person who gave me the collection had gone on the same retreat a few years prior and had given me the collection when he returned. Looking back, I should have thrown it away, but I still had a lot of growing to do.) The realization that God was watching everything I was doing gave me the desire to do better. It did not matter if I was fooling my wife and children, family, friends, or co-workers; God could see everything I was doing. After this weekend, I tried to live like He was right there with me, but I still fell short often.

Another change occurred in our business. At our first meeting after the retreat, I shared the secrets of success with our agents and gave them the tools. I had never been completely honest with them about how God had blessed me. I let them know that God had been the reason for my success and that He had blessed me more than I deserved. I shared that I wasn't really anyone special, but I wanted to start thanking God and beginning our meetings with prayer. It was the first time I had ever prayed in front of anyone, and I got stuck halfway through the prayer. I just couldn't speak, and there was a long, awkward silence. Then I said, "In Jesus's name, amen."

There were mixed emotions about the prayer at the meeting. Many of our team members were very supportive, but one team member acted like he was going to run out of the room. Ultimately, it did not matter what anyone thought about praying at the meeting. I felt this was what God wanted me to do.

As soon as we started praying, the trials began. We had an agent die in a car accident, and another left after a dispute with a fellow agent. My partner started working for another agency and recruiting agents away from our own company. We completed the office building, but agent after agent transferred to other firms or dropped out of the business completely. The road was getting bumpy, but my faith grew tremendously.

We were attending church faithfully, and I began having Bible studies at my home before the weekly card game. We started reading *The Purpose Driven Life* as a group, and slowly, one by one, my card-playing friends quit coming. By the end of the forty-chapter forty-week book, we were down to a few guys who just came because of Bible study and did not want to play cards. One such person was Rodney with the Fellowship of Christian Athletes, who reached out to me because I coached middle school soccer. I was fortunate to coach the boys and girls' teams. Both teams were very competitive, and we had winning records every year. I was pretty intense as a coach and pushed the kids to run hard. I would always run with them and push them to go faster.

Going into 2008, with encouragement from Coach Rodney from FCA, I began to pray with the teams I coached, and the following year, we started a coaches' Bible study. We had about ten coaches to start, but before the next year's seasons began, every one of the coaches in our study had been terminated except for me, and I was only volunteering at this point. The athletic director who had hired these coaches had died of cancer, and the new AD let them go one by one. We had coach after coach leave the program, and as our children went from middle school to high school, many student athletes left our home district for school choice. As a result, only three of us finished the study. One night, we talked about baptism and realized none of our trio had been baptized. After some discussion, we decided to go to my house and get baptized in the river. My fellow coaches and my wife, Leigh Ann, all decided to get baptized at nine o'clock at night.

The next day, I went to work as usual. One of our agents had spilled a cup of coffee into her purse, and her belongings were spread across the counter, drying out. When I asked what happened, she replied that she was having a rough time and didn't know what else to do. I asked if she had tried praying. She replied that she would try anything at this point. I prayed with her, and for her, she cried, and I could feel the Holy

Spirit. She gave her life to Christ and became a much stronger person. It wasn't that her life became perfect, but she was able to deal with her imperfect life while walking with a perfect Savior.

While my faith was growing and we were getting by a day at a time, Chuck was crashing harder and harder. One day, I heard him and his wife, Tina, fighting from the backyard. She was screaming for help, so I ran into the house. She was holding up a chair to protect herself. He was pretty lit up and not in a talking mood. I can't remember what she said, but he ran at her, and she smacked him with the chair. He hit the bottom of the chair with his legs, which caused the top of the chair to pivot and hit him in the forehead. It broke the chair, and he fell to the ground. I picked him up off the floor and took him to the sink. As he bled, I joked with him and said, "Man, that was a bad idea."

I asked Leigh Ann to bring a Bible over to the house. When things calmed down, we talked and prayed together. The next day, I saw Tina in her backyard. She said, "Do you see that?" while pointing at our house.

I said, "No."

She said, "Come here." I walked next door and looked back, and there was a rainbow coming out of the roof of our home and ending on the other side of the river. The rainbow stayed for a long time. We went out in the river and took pictures. Tina came to church that weekend, and Chuck did, as well, for a couple of weeks. Unfortunately, he did not come for long, as he preferred to "worship" in the casino.

The financial crisis hit them hard as well, but the drugs, drinking, and gambling sped up the process. As my priorities continued to change, I quit taking Chuck to the bars and encouraged him to come to church and AA. The more I pressed him to do the right thing, the more he ran the other way.

By now, Chuck and Tina's son, Aaron, was in the sixth grade and playing soccer on the middle school team I coached. Mechanically gifted, Aaron had racked up a room full of motocross trophies, but even though he could drive anything, he wasn't the most gifted athletically. His motocross number was 717, so he begged me to have the number 17 for his soccer jersey. The number had special significance to Aaron because seventeen was his dad's number when he played lacrosse in high school, and Chuck's birthday was the 17th of June. I explained to Aaron that the older kids get first pick on jersey numbers, but he was a lot like his dad in many ways, always trying to make a deal. He told me he would run extra laps if he could have number seventeen, so I let him. He ran the extra laps, and I hid the shirt till after practice.

While Aaron was respectful to others, he was often a brat toward his parents and would throw a fit if he didn't get what he wanted from them. He was also showing signs of Tourette's syndrome. Chuck would give him anything he wanted to make him happy. He bought him a Bobcat when he was around eleven years old, and Aaron started building a motocross track in their backyard. It was cool for him, but it got on our nerves pretty quickly. One day, while we were having guests over for a cookout, Aaron started riding his motocross bike in the backyard. I asked him to go ride elsewhere for a while, and his parents backed me up. He had a fit. When he flew into rages, his Tourette's would really start acting up. He began taking medication for the twitches and nervous ticks he was having.

Their family was falling apart, and I kept trying to stop the train wreck of my best friend's life, but he wasn't listening. As bills were piling up, Chuck kept going to the casino. One night, Tina called and asked me to go get him. Sure enough, there was Chuck, drunk and swaying in front of a slot machine. I told him that Tina had asked me to go pick him up and had also shared that the mortgage had not been paid in months. When I tried to get him to leave, he got angry and told me to leave him alone. I reached out and gave him a tug on the elbow and tried to coax him again since he was doing his best to ignore me and kept putting money in the slot machine. He pulled away and then took a swing at me. He was drunk, so it was in slow motion. He missed, and I grabbed him by the sleeves of his jacket as he kept trying to hit me and couldn't. He then yelled for security.

When security arrived, Chuck told them I was harassing him and should leave. I explained to the security guard that my friend was drunk and losing his house and family. Enraged with my interference, he started punching the slot machine. I asked security if he could kick Chuck out for what he was doing. The security guard went to the slot machine and asked him to stop, or he would have to leave. He stopped and asked the security guard to have me removed from the casino. The security guard came back to me and said I didn't have to leave, but I could not bother Chuck, and if I did, he would call the police. I then told the security guard that I understood why; having drunk people blow their mortgage payments in the slot machine was job security. I left disgusted, told Tina and my wife what happened, and went to bed.

The next day, I got a call from a friend who told me that Chuck claimed he broke his hand punching me in the face. I just laughed and shared the truth. I saw Chuck later in the week with a brace on his hand from punching the slot machine. I really felt sorry for him and his wife and children. He was losing everything yet kept going back to the source of his own demise. He could not stay sober and could not tell the truth either.

A couple of weeks after the casino incident, Chuck left for Florida and told Tina he was not coming back. He wasn't speaking to me, and Tina and I were lost about what else we could do. He had been crashing for several years now, and he had rejected every attempt to help him. We decided to pray for him on a Thursday night when no one else was at the church.

The morning of the prayer session, I met with some men at Teen Challenge for a monthly chapel service where I would share testimony and have them share a scripture with me. One of the men shared Proverbs 17:17 (HCSB), which says, "A friend loves at all times and a brother is born for a time of need." That morning, when I left the chapel service, I texted the scripture to Chuck, knowing it would mean something to him because of the number seventeen. We hadn't spoken in about a month, and he was still in Florida. He called me a minute after I sent the text and apologized, but then he went on to say that he just wanted to do what he wanted to do. I was glad he called and told him I still loved him and would be there for him when he needed me because a friend loves at all times, and a brother is born for a time of need.

That night, we gathered about a dozen of his closest family and friends to pray for him at the altar. Aaron was there running around the church like a normal kid. I noticed that his Tourette's was not acting up at all, which was unusual because his symptoms had been getting worse all the time. We formed a circle. Everyone took a turn praying. Tina and I cried out to God, and He heard our prayer. The presence of the Holy Spirit was as strong as anything I had ever felt. After we were done praying, I felt a huge weight was lifted, and Tina felt the same. We knew that Chuck wasn't healed yet, but we also knew that God was going to take care of him and that we had done what we could. We left the church floating on a cloud.

When we got home, Tina brought over some pie and shared what an incredible experience she had at the church and that she felt a thousand times lighter. I felt the same and told her about the verse and talking to Chuck.

I then asked her where Aaron was, and she told me he was next door working on a school project. I asked her if I could go tell him about speaking to Chuck and share the verse with him. She said, "Of course," and I went to see him.

When I walked into their living room, Aaron was on the floor working on a big red trifold project board. He had pictures and articles all over the board, and I began to ask him about the project. He told me that his assignment was to do a project about a particular disease, and he wanted to do his on Tourette's. He also shared with me that he had traded with someone to get the project because he had Tourette's, and so did his favorite motocross racer, who was nicknamed Twitch because of his spasms. He had a picture of Twitch flying through the air on a motorcycle on the board with some other articles.

Aaron's Tourette's was really acting up while he was telling me about his project. His whole body was clinching like he had palsy, and his eyes were rolling back in his head like he was having a seizure, but he was speaking normally. It was painful to watch him go through this torment on top of everything else going on in his life. I had never seen his Tourette's cause him so much discomfort.

Then I asked him why there were pictures of the devil and demons on his board. While he was having spasms and clenching his entire body, he told me that the demons were on the board because people used to think when you had Tourette's, you were possessed by the devil.

At that moment, the hairs on my neck stood up, and I felt an evil presence like I had never experienced before. I then told Aaron about talking to his dad and the scripture Proverbs 17:17. I opened up the Bible that Leigh Ann had brought to their house and handed it to Aaron. I asked him to read the verse, and when I handed him the Bible, I said a silent prayer: "God, help this boy, and devil, leave this boy alone!" Instantly, his body relaxed, and the Tourette's was gone. He read the verse, and his symptoms never returned. I went home, freaked out a little, and told my wife what happened. I asked her if she thought I was crazy, and she said she believed me but that I probably shouldn't tell anyone.

That same night, I went to sleep and had a dream that I was doing an open house, and this gothic-looking couple came into the house and asked me how business was going. It was around 2008, so I replied that it could be better, but we were paying the bills. Then, I asked them how their business was going. They replied, "Business has never been better. We are devouring souls!" Suddenly, they put a Darth Vader-type death grip on my neck and chest, and I couldn't breathe. They weren't touching me, but I was fighting for my life. I was choking to death. My heart was pounding faster than I had ever felt it, and I thought I was about to die. Then I raised my hand in the air and said, "I rebuke this in the name of Jesus," and I woke up instantly. My hand was still in the air. I was drenched in a pool of sweat, my heart was still racing, and I was still gasping for air. I reached over, and Leigh Ann was still beside me, and everything was okay. I just kept saying "Thank You, Jesus" over and over because I felt like my life was just spared.

Exhausted, I went back to sleep and dreamed I was floating through the roof of our home, where the rainbow had just been shining, and into the clouds toward a bright light shining behind a cross. I was tingling all over and kept getting closer and closer to God. It was a glimpse of heaven, and I did not want to wake up. Eventually, I did, and I told Leigh Ann about my dream the next day. I asked her again if she thought I was crazy. She said she knew I was crazy but loved me anyway and that I probably shouldn't tell anyone about this, either.

We watched Aaron for a year or more and never saw the Tourette's again. Eventually, I asked him what happened to his Tourette's, and he told me it just went away. I asked him if he was still taking medication for it, and he was not. Some may say it's a coincidence. I say miracles do happen.

The night after learning that Aaron was cured, we took the kids on a youth group trip. I have a hard time keeping a secret, so I shared the story with a good friend who went on the trip with us. I am not sure if I told him about the encounter with Aaron, but I definitely told him about the dream I had. When we went to the main event of the night, a pastor shared Psalm 91:1–16:

> *Whoever dwells in the shelter of the Most High will rest in the shadow of the Almighty. I will say of the Lord, "He is my refuge and my fortress, my God, in whom I trust." Surely he will save you from the fowler's snare and from the deadly pestilence. He will cover you with his feathers, and under his wings you will find refuge; his faithfulness will be your shield and rampart. You will not fear the terror of night, nor the arrow that flies by day, nor the pestilence that stalks in the darkness, nor the plague that destroys at midday. A thousand may fall at your side, ten thousand at your right hand, but it will not come near you. You will only observe with your eyes and see the punishment of the wicked. If you say, "The Lord is my refuge," and you make the Most High your dwelling, no harm will overtake you, no disaster will come near your tent. For he will command his angels concerning you to guard you in all your ways; they will lift you up in their hands, so that you will not strike your foot against a stone. You will tread on the lion and the cobra; you will trample the great lion and the serpent. "Because he loves me," says the Lord, "I will rescue him; I will protect him, for he acknowledges my name. He will call on me, and I will answer him; I will be with him in trouble, I will deliver him and honor*

> *him. With long life I will satisfy him and show him my salvation."*
>
> — Psalm 91:1–16 (NIV)

After this was shared, my friend and I looked at each other, and I was amazed at how God was speaking to me so clearly through this verse.

At the rally, I was rooming with another good friend, Thunder, the banker. We served together in the Lion's Club and went to church together. Thunder and Michael, the schoolteacher, have always been great friends. They have always been hard-working, faithful husbands and fathers. We had the privilege of sponsoring both of them on the church retreat, and they were greatly impacted in a positive spiritual way. The difference in their lives was not as dramatic as mine because they were already living the right way, but you could see a change as they both began to study the Word more and serve in church. Michael began to sing in the praise team.

So, back to the night after the rally. This was the next night after I had the dream with the demons and the cross. We put all the kids to bed, and Thunder and I went back to the room to crash. I was exhausted. I fell asleep and began to dream about my wife. I started to rub her back and then lifted up her shirt and went underneath. I woke up when I felt hair under my hand. Thank God Thunder had a hairy back and a sense of humor because I was about to reach around the front! Anyway, we both laugh about that moment to this day. The next night, we put a wall of pillows between us, and I slept on top of the sheet while he slept under.

The kids had a great time, and we went to the youth rallies for many years.

Meanwhile, Chuck kept crashing in every way. Although he eventually returned from Florida, he only continued his downward spiral.

Another couple of years passed, and Tina left. After that, Chuck went off the rails even more. There was all kinds of drug activity next door. One day, I caught Aaron smoking weed in the basement. He was fourteen years old, and when I told Chuck, he really didn't care and said Aaron probably got it from him. He was only upset that Aaron was using his bong. Aaron and Chuck began to avoid me, and I didn't mind because I was fed up with the shenanigans. We had to forbid our children from going over there, and once they realized what was going on, they really didn't want to be around them. I continued to pray for Chuck and call periodically to let him know that I still loved him and there was a better way, but I was relieved in a way that he had become distant.

Chuck had maxed out every credit card and line of credit and blown through hundreds of thousands of dollars, eventually filing bankruptcy. I helped him and Tina do a short sale on the house. Once the house sold, we did not see each other as much or talk for a while.

By this time, Chuck had been seriously injured in a motocross accident that resulted in a metal collar bone and a shoulder that was, as he put it, held together with screws and rubber bands. As the oxycodone epidemic took hold, the pill mills and doctors cut back on Chuck's pills, and his addiction turned to heroin. Then I saw him on the news one night. He was arrested for taking his son to a drug deal. Aaron was now in high school, and the party lifestyle was what he knew. I would see Aaron at school and try to convince him to come to FCA, but he was not interested. Soon after, Chuck got arrested for stealing a checkbook from one of the girlfriends he had after the divorce.

A few months after that, I got a call from a friend who saw Chuck in a car crash on the side of the road. When I went to see him at the hospital, there were needle marks on his arms, and he was in and out of consciousness. His girlfriend at the time was a high school teacher named Christine. She was a super sweet person and initially was pretty naive to what Chuck was doing. When I suggested that she give him the ultimatum of Teen Challenge or rehab rather than continue to live in her home, Chuck chose jail because his DUIs had caught up with him. It was clear he was not ready for suggestions.

I let it go for a time since our family was having its own issues.

As my son became a freshman in high school, he started to slack off on his schoolwork and became disrespectful to his mother. For the first time in his life, he got a D on his report card. She did a little research on teenage boys and discovered that this is common; young men do not want to listen to women, so fathers need to take a more active role. She challenged me to step up and make sure he did his homework and was more respectful to her. We had a few knock-down, drag-out fights, but he eventually came around, and it was worth the effort. When he would not cooperate at home, I went to the school and asked for a meeting with me and his guidance counselors.

This was always beneficial, as sometimes we needed a mediator to keep our tempers in check.

We also used parental controls on the cell phone when our children did not listen. We would shut them down so they could only communicate with us and a small list of trusted numbers. We would shut down the internet access as well.

Teenage attitudes aside, both of our children worked very hard academically and athletically. As a result, they were honor society students and all-state athletes. It did not come naturally; both of them were smaller than their teammates, but they had a drive, desire, and competitiveness that made them great leaders in their respective sports. Both were varsity captains and state qualifiers in multiple sports while maintaining GPAs ranking in the top ten in their classes.

I was very proud of them, but even more so when it came to their influence on their peers in a spiritual sense. They would faithfully attend huddles of the Fellowship of Christian Athletes (FCA) and would invite their friends to come. They were great children but far from perfect, just as I was far from a perfect parent, but they knew that Jesus was there for us when we needed strength and forgiveness. They saw their mother and I fight like cats and dogs, but they also saw us reconcile and pray to be better spouses and parents.

During my son's freshman year of high school, we were holding FCA huddles for each of the teams at the high school. We were meeting with each team after school on a different day. One day, while waiting for the basketball to come into the huddle room, one of the players exchanged words with another kid in the hallway. I stepped in between, and the basketball player came to the huddle. After some discussion, I found out that he was a believer and had memorized the Twenty-Third Psalm. I went home that day and began to pray about how we could reach the entire school. The idea came to me about having a Christmas rally where students would share testimonies, lead worship, perform skits, and receive Jesus. It was about one week before Christmas, and I was praying for God to confirm that this was what He wanted done. I was getting up the nerve to call the school to ask for permission to use the gym for this rally. I went to pray and opened up my Bible to Matthew 7:7. I did not have a verse in mind; I just opened the Bible, and this verse came up, which reads, "Ask, and it shall be given you; seek, and you shall find; knock, and it shall be opened unto you" (Matthew 7:7, NIV). Once I read this verse, I knew this was what God wanted, but I still did not make the call.

All day, I was wrestling with my fears; they would not allow the event in a public school, the students would not share or come, and my kids would be embarrassed by my outward expression of faith. Later that afternoon, while I continued to pray and wrestle, I received a text from a friend who would send a group text with a daily scripture. This scripture on this day was Matthew 7:7. I got chills and knew I had to make the call. The principal was open, and we set the date. I met with the teams, and several of them stepped up to do music, testimony, and skits. Even the athletic director agreed to give each student a free pass to a sporting event at the school.

And you know what? The event was awesome. We had about two hundred students attend. Big Mack, who was the senior class president, shared how God saved him from suicide and how he grew from the chubby kid that everyone picked on to be a star athlete and class president. Another student shared how one of his brothers was in jail, and another was killed, but his faith in God kept him from going down the wrong road. The student who almost got in the fight the week before recited the Twenty-Third Psalm from memory. Our guest speaker was Coach Rodney, the FCA director. He gave an invitation to receive Christ, and all two hundred students accepted Jesus or recommitted their faith. It was an incredible experience, and the atmosphere of the school changed. We gave out FCA T-shirts, which read "Competitor for Christ." They were worn proudly as our students found their identity in Jesus and not in the result on the scoreboard.

Every team began to pray together before and after games and invited their opponents to pray, as well. It was a moving sight to see teams of young people gathered at midfield or center court praying together.

It was rare, but there were times when some athletes did not participate, and a couple of times, entire teams were told they could not pray by their coaches. This is a clear violation of the constitutional right to freedom of religious expression. No one can force someone to pray, but likewise, no one can deny the right of someone to pray. While coaching my daughter's middle school soccer team, I saw this happen more than once. One team in particular was playing music before the game. The song "Highway to Hell" was blaring as the coach told their athletes they were not allowed to pray with our team. Our girls were extremely talented, and after we scored about five goals, one of the girls on the other team said, "We should have prayed."

Unfortunately, there was pushback from the administration and school board members. I was told that we could not do what we were doing because there was a separation of church and state. I did my homework and met with a good friend who lobbied for religious freedoms. She also gave me materials to use from the Alliance Defense Fund, which explained the rights of students to participate in and lead religious activities in public schools. I stood up against the pushback, and when we were told that FCA could not hold a baccalaureate service for the graduating seniors, I told the superintendent to check with the school attorney and get back to me. Once he verified that he could not legally stop this event, we had an incredibly moving experience with dozens of students coming to the cross on the altar we placed on the auditorium stage.

The apex of the event was a drama performed by the students where not a word was spoken. It is on YouTube called "Lifehouse's Everything Skit." It begins with a girl standing lifeless, and then Jesus comes and breathes life into her. He shows her the world and begins to dance with her. Then, a boy comes to interrupt, pulls her from Jesus, and begins to dance with her. Jesus is pushed aside by the boy and stands waiting in the background. Next, a girl comes with a bottle to pull the girl away from the boy and drinks with her. The girl gets further from Jesus as she does this. Another boy comes to give the girl gifts and money, and the girl grabs them as the gap between her and Jesus grows. The wall of people and temptations pile up. Another girl comes and shows her how to walk and dress like a model, also showing her how to throw up to stay thin. Finally, a demon covered in black comes prowling with a knife and shows her how to cut herself. As she is doing this, he throws her to the floor and puts a gun in her hand. As she kneels in tears, Jesus falls to His knees to pray for her, and she throws the gun and rushes toward Him. The people who led her away from Jesus hold her back from Him, throwing her down over and over, but she persists, and Jesus jumps between them and the girl, throwing them to the ground. He picks her up and brushes her off, and they dance again.

The auditorium exploded with emotion. There were cheers and tears, and there was no room on the altar for all of the students kneeling around the cross. It was a beautiful moment that I will cherish forever.

The faith of the school grew as our efforts with FCA continued, and students became empowered by Jesus. But the following year, the pushback started again. I received several reprimands from school administrators for encouraging prayer, meeting with students, and giving out Bibles on school grounds. I received a call from a school board member saying we could no longer hold "revivals" in the high school. It was at that moment that I decided to run for school board against this man. I prayed for confirmation, and it was made clear to me during my prayer that I would win with 70 percent of the vote. I told my good friend Michael about this confirmation. He was a teacher, and we coached together for many years. Our children grew up together, and his wife and mine were close friends as well. He was surprised by my prediction; being a math teacher, he predicted a close race, maybe 55 to 45. After all, I was still an ex-convict with no college degree and no experience in education. I campaigned heavily, toured schools, met with community leaders to gain support and put up signs all over the district.

I won with 70 percent of the vote.

A large majority of people I met with shared that it was time for the superintendent to retire. He had been in this position for thirty-four years, and the district was suffering due to students leaving for greener pastures and other districts. School choice began to negatively impact our local district as parents chose tech, charter, and neighboring districts in huge numbers. It was heartbreaking to see our children and teams split apart after eighth grade. As I became vocal about the inequities and segregation that was occurring because of school choice, I was accused of being a racist for noticing the White flight occurring in our community. Meanwhile, our children stayed in the local district and thrived academically, athletically, and socially.

At my first school board meeting, after being sworn in, I said the Lord's Prayer during the moment of silence. I was reprimanded yet again, but I continued to pray at future meetings. Members of the public came out in support. I was even on local TV sharing my opinion on prayer. I was determined to pray even under protest. We eventually compromised to allow a time of prayer before the meeting where people could come before the public session began.

Once I shared the consensus of the community that it was time for a new superintendent, I became a target by the current super. I had a disagreement with the athletic director, who let go of all of the excellent coaches from our Bible study. He replaced them with very inexperienced and unskilled coaches. Our athletic teams began to struggle, and I told him I was not going to support his poor decisions on the board. As the enemy of the super and the AD, three board members voted to censure me. This was done by drafting multiple statements of untruth with allegations ranging from intimidating staff members because of my disagreement with the AD to using my position for personal financial gain because teachers and admin used my real estate company to buy, sell, and rent houses. It was a smear campaign that was designed to discredit me and even get me removed from the board.

I feel it important to mention that being a board member was a volunteer position. There was no pay for the countless hours meeting with the board, students, and staff, coaching, volunteering, or giving rides because there was no activity bus for the students. Most of the students whose parents could afford cars for their kids had choiced out of the district, and most of the students who were left had to work to pay for a cell phone or save for a car. Most of the kids on the teams did not have parents come to watch them play.

To help make up for these inequities, my wife and I became the booster presidents for many of the booster programs at the school. Meanwhile, my daughter's swim team went from seventy students her freshman year to six her senior year. My son's wrestling team went from an integrated team his freshman year to a 90 percent minority by the time he was a senior. I heard many parents asking why I would keep my kids in "that" place with "those" kids.

My business began to suffer even more because of my absence and dedication to the school district. I was criticized for being too involved by my agents, clients, and even my children. Several more agents left our company, and I was hanging on by a thread. We were barely making payroll; we were not going on vacations; we stopped eating out. Leigh was in tears many days because we were going into such a financial hole. We were basically keeping the business afloat with equity loans from the properties we had acquired.

A few agents did stand by us through thick and thin. One agent in particular, Terry, who has been with me since we opened our company, is a great man of God and a blessing in my life. During this time, when we were really struggling, I asked him if things could get any worse. He replied, "What are you talking about? You are not hanging from a cross." I immediately had a different perspective on life. I often struggled with the crucifixion and wondered why a loving God would let His own Son suffer in such a gruesome way. Once Terry made this statement, it became clear that God let this occur so we would not have an excuse to feel sorry for whatever our situation. No matter what we are going through, it pales in comparison to the torture Jesus endured. He was slapped and beaten, spit upon, stripped naked, His flesh ripped from His body, hung on a cross, speared in His side, and bled to death, and I was upset that I might not be able to pay for my million-dollar home. The greatest man to walk the face of the earth was homeless. It was one of the greatest *aha* moments of my life. From this day forward, I have had some bad days, but the thought of Jesus on the cross has always made my trials seem easier.

Shortly after that revelation, we received a call from a city code enforcement officer. One of our rental properties had a sewer backup, and the house was condemned. We were only a year away from paying off the mortgage.

Our debt was choking us, and I did not have the money to pay someone to fix the problem, so I decided to fix it myself. I put on work clothes and opened the crawl space door, only to find that the crawl space was filled with sewage. I almost threw up and just said, "God, please help me out. We need a break." I surrendered emotionally and spiritually, but I really did not know what to do next.

I went to catch my breath, literally and figuratively, and at just that moment, my wife pulled up in the driveway, honking the horn and smiling brightly while waving an envelope. When I asked her what was going on, she showed me a commission check for $36,000. I was completely shocked and questioned her about how we received this check for such a large amount of money. At first, I was in disbelief; then, she explained that an agent had sold a million-dollar property and never turned in the contract, so we had no idea this was coming.

Once I understood what had happened, I became overwhelmed with emotion and gratitude. Tears came to my eyes, and I knew God had answered my prayer. Since that day, I have never doubted that God would provide for us and do so abundantly. I called a plumber, and he sent a camera down the sewer line. It turned out that the gas company had run a new gas main through our sewer line. The gas company cleaned up the mess and paid a plumber to fix the pipe. The condemnation was lifted, and we continued to work through our financial problems.

I spent many Sundays at the altar asking God to help me with my finances, and He always came through. I kept serving

Him, and He kept providing, even when people doubted we would make it through the recession. I was also able to hire an attorney to get the school board censure revoked and removed from the school board website. I was not removed from the board, and every time I was attacked, I just remembered what Jesus went through and trusted that God would not give me more than I could handle.

There were several times during this period when I considered selling the business and going back to sales or just running the property management business. One time in particular, I was on the phone with a competitor, and we were getting pretty close to coming to terms on merging offices. Just when I thought we were about to close the deal, our walls started moving in the office. I was alarmed and told him what was happening, and he shared that his walls were moving as well. We both said at the same time, "I will call you back." It was as if God was not happy with our conversation or the thought of me selling the company. It was the first earthquake I had ever experienced, and I think we both considered it a sign to wait and see.

Meanwhile, back on the school board, it took a few years, but we eventually hired a new superintendent, and it was a breath of fresh air. He was a great man of God and completely supported our efforts with FCA. We went from meeting after school to meeting during lunch, and FCA grew. Our rallies went from after school to during the day as an optional event. In my daughter's senior year, we had most of the school attend, and her good friends shared testimony at both of the rallies we held. The response was incredible; hundreds of students came to Christ.

One of the testimonies just before Christmas was from Sherry, a state champion track athlete, 1,000-point basketball star, and lettered in six varsity sports her senior year. Hailey lettered in six sports as well. They were great friends, exemplary students, and extraordinary examples to underclassmen. As team captains and leaders in sobriety and faith, they led prayers and shared Christ with teammates and the school. Sherry shared about the first time she felt the presence of God with hundreds of students, and you could have heard a pin drop. She was so loved and respected by the entire school and staff that everyone wanted to hear what she had to say. Students wanted what she had and came forward to find out more about Jesus.

At the next rally during Easter, we had another incredible event and testimony from another one of Hailey's great friends. Sarah had a different story than Sherry but just as powerful. Tears came as she shared her feelings of self-doubt, which led to drinking and depression, thoughts of being lost, and even suicidal ideation. First, she shared these thoughts privately with Hailey, and this was when Hailey introduced her to Jesus. Sarah recalled the conversation publicly with hundreds of her classmates. Hailey told her, "That is what Jesus is for. He loves us and forgives us, and we can lean on Him when we fall short or feel less than." The message of God's love and forgiveness was felt, and once again, hundreds of students came to know Christ that day.

It was an absolutely incredible movement and a time I will never forget. I felt that we had finally accomplished what God wanted: students in a public school freely expressing their love for God and belief in Jesus during the school day.

I couldn't wait for the baccalaureate service and the next rally, but the enemy was prowling. It wasn't long after this rally that there was gay pride day at the school. I was in the cafeteria, as I often visited with students and invited them to attend FCA meetings and rallies. Two of my daughter's childhood friends opposed what we were doing, as they knew where I stood on issues of homosexuality.

One of the girls had a mother who had left her husband for another woman. The girl's father had been one of my best friends for years. We had coached together, played cards together, and taken many trips to the island and other vacations together. He was an atheist, and we would often debate religion and the existence of God. One night, we debated after a card game till two in the morning. Finally, after neither of us was budging on our position, I asked him to pray about anything and see what happened.

My son and his son were friends, as well, and Zak went to spend the night at his house. When they arrived at the house, it had been weeks since their trash was picked up. He had canceled trash service years before, but they never came and picked up the container and continued to pick up his trash, so he had free trash service. Eventually, they figured out that he was not getting a bill or paying for service, so they stopped picking up the trash. After our debate, he, his son, and my son went to the pile of trash and prayed, "God, if You are real, pick up my trash tomorrow. Amen."

The next morning, they woke up, and the trash was gone, and so were his containers. He called to tell me right away, and I said, "I told you so." He still argued that if God really loved him, He would have left the cans. I just laughed and said, "God wants you to know that He is real and that He does not want you to steal."

We were great friends and still are, but our friendship was tested when his daughter began to bash my daughter and our family for our beliefs. She became rude and condescending toward our whole family, and during the gay pride day at the school, she asked me if I liked her shirt, knowing where I stood on the matter. It was rainbow tie dye and said, "Closets are for clothes."

Making a crude joke, I said, "Yeah, and queers." Some of the other students heard me and laughed. Her reply was that she couldn't believe I would come at her family like that. I was instantly regretful. I knew I was wrong. I was not even thinking about her mom when I made the comment. I was disappointed in myself, and that comment hurt this girl who was already struggling in so many ways. I made the comment in passing and was immediately convicted to turn around and apologize. I immediately reached out to her father, the principal, the superintendent, and the school board president to explain my lapse in judgment and apologized to them for what may come from this.

The girl rejected my apology and told her mother. Her mother messaged me and was irate, claiming I said something even more derogatory. So I tried to explain and apologized again. I offered to meet with her to discuss the matter in detail, and she refused. She filed a complaint with the superintendent, but nothing permanently or immediately came from the matter.

While Hailey was very adamant about herself not drinking and doing drugs, her friends had started to fall victim to the party lifestyle. Hailey would spend nights alone at home because she was not included in the party plans. Hailey would tell us what was going on, and I would reach out to parents to let them know what their kids were doing. Some parents were grateful, but a couple of parents accused me and Hailey of lying. One parent became so irate they yelled at me on the phone. Six months later, the girls whose parents accused us of lying were arrested for possession of marijuana.

One of the gay pride groups of girls that was and still is close with Hailey decided to throw a party in a vacant home in our community. These same girls had developed code words for getting high, like "having mac and cheese," so Hailey would not know what they were planning. The home in question was a doctor's home—over 10,000 square feet—in foreclosure and had been vacant for a year or more. One night, we were coming home and saw cryptic signs in the neighborhood saying to park here and follow the signs. I saw a bunch of my daughter's friends walking down the street toward this home. The signs led directly to the vacant house. The kids decided to blaze it up. Once I discovered what was going on, I called the police and went to the house to bust up the party. The kids came pouring out of the house like someone had tipped them off. I found out later that it was Hailey. I also discovered that she had been at the house but left when the partying started. She even let them use our sound system for the event.

There were probably one hundred or more kids in this house. It reminded me of my younger days when I was planning the big drunk fest with all my friends in high school. Now, I was the old jerk calling the cops.

As the kids came out of the house, there were many I recognized who were just at the rally a few weeks prior. Some attended FCA, and now they were hanging out in a vacant home, many of them drinking and getting high. One of them yelled from a distance, "F#%& you, Frank Parks!"

That same night, there was another party going on down the road from our house next to a piece of land that we owned, so unintentionally, I broke up that party as well because they freaked out when all the cop cars went flying by. Needless to say, my and my daughter's names were mud in school on Monday. She was harassed to the point of tears. Fortunately for the students, Hailey saved them by telling them the police were coming, but that did not matter. According to the kids in school, I was the worst for breaking up the party, and Hailey had heard enough.

I went to meet with the school resource officer and showed him all of the evidence compiled, most of it from social media. The kids had posted pictures from the party, videos of them making alcohol punch, and cryptic instructions on how to get to the party. I asked him not to arrest them but to put the fear of God into them and to make them quit harassing my daughter. Many of the students came to apologize, but not the one girl who put the whole plan together. She continued to deny her involvement, and her parents covered for her in spite of the evidence I showed them and the police officer. I should have pressed to have her arrested, but instead, she was benched for a game on the soccer team while her mom berated me because my daughter was still playing.

At the next board meeting, a group of five parents showed up to complain about my "abuse of authority" for telling the school resource officer about something that did not happen on school grounds. They insinuated that Hailey was guilty as well and had received preferential treatment because I was on the board. Hailey had lied to me about being at the party, but she was home when I arrived at 10 p.m. I am pretty sure she was the only one punished once I found out she was there. The parents, one by one, shared their opinion that I had overstepped my bounds as a school board member and that I should not be allowed to volunteer. Going into the cafeteria was mentioned as a problem as well.

Once they were done with their public comments, I asked for a few minutes to respond. I shared that the reason I went to the school resource officer was that my daughter was being bullied because I broke up the party where these students had broken into a vacant home to drink underage and get high. I also pointed out how disgraceful it was for these parents to reprimand me when their children were breaking the law and could have been arrested. One of the fathers, who used to be my friend, interrupted, stating, "This is not the place for this discussion."

I replied, "Well, then you should have thought about that before you brought it here." It was amazing to see them bash me and my daughter, but when I brought the truth to the table, they didn't want to hear what I had to say. I was beginning to feel more like Jesus all the time. He was not respected in his hometown either.

In spite of the controversy, we held the baccalaureate and continued with FCA meetings. Participation declined, though. The following year, I passed the FCA torch to the football coach, who wanted to have meetings in the morning before school. I still had some connection with the students, but it was not the same as the lifelong relationships I had with my children's classmates. While a few relationships had soured, the good far outweighed the bad.

Over the years since they graduated high school, many of my children's classmates have reached out to me for guidance on spiritual matters and recovery. Some are still in recovery and attending church, as well.

One student-athlete whom I coached came to see us when his girlfriend was pregnant. She was considering an abortion and had a fear of raising a child as a single mother. He wanted her to have the baby but did not want to make the commitment of marriage. I shared my experience with abortion and also shared how I was not willing to commit to marriage when I was his age, either. We counseled them on what God would want them to do and that He doesn't make mistakes. Before they left, she agreed to keep the child, and he agreed to step up to be a godly husband. They got married, and he joined the military. He is a Marine now, and they have had more children. I see him sharing posts about his family often, and I am grateful for the relationship God gave us and that our position on abortion has changed. It is heartwarming to see them with their children.

As for the two parents who were most adamant that their children were not getting high—those were the two girls who were arrested shortly after graduation. It was tragic and just what I was trying to prevent. Part of me wanted to call the parents and say, "I told you so," but I prayed for them instead.

My daughter is still close with one of the girls, and she still struggles. I pray for freedom and salvation in her life.

I am incredibly proud of Hailey for remaining a loyal and faithful friend, even when she has been ridiculed and betrayed. She shows love and compassion to everyone and is an inspiration for sobriety in young people. She has dealt with some tough losses. Several of her friends have died suddenly and tragically, but she continues to be a bright light wherever she goes.

I have seen many young people lose the battle to addiction, and it is the most heartbreaking thing to experience. There are several young men I coached or mentored who have died from using. Every time a death occurs, I feel defeated for a moment, and then I get motivated to do more to reach the lost and broken.

My school board term ended the year after my daughter graduated. There were more changes to the staff and board. While trying to plan a rally, I went to the school to get kids to sign up in the cafeteria, as I had done for many years. I was stopped at the main office and told the principal would like to talk to me. As I waited in the principal's office, I had flashbacks of when I was in school and knew I was in trouble. The principal came in with another administrator to tell me that club activities were no longer allowed during the school day, even at lunchtime. I protested as we had been having FCA rallies for years and always gotten students to sign up during lunch. They said we could use the school announcements only, which were not effective. I asked them what would happen if I went into the cafeteria without their permission. They replied that they would call the police. For a moment, I considered going in protest and getting arrested. Then, I remembered the lies that were told previously by the board members and how they would stretch this one if the police were involved. In a disgusted tone, I told them that I had never been more disappointed in the school leadership than I was on that day. Not only would they have to answer to me and the students who were being denied their First Amendment freedoms, but ultimately, they would have to answer to God for what they had done.

I left the school very sad and heartbroken, as I knew many students would miss out on a chance to know Christ. I considered suing the district but ultimately took it as a sign from God that my season there had ended. I introduced FCA staff members to the coaches and began to spend more time serving with the church retreat and going to recovery meetings.

CHAPTER 12:

Becoming a Fisherman

In 2009, I had the opportunity to serve on a church retreat weekend. After attending the initial weekend, participants can return to serve the next group. While serving on the kitchen crew, I met a brother in Christ who inspired me to do what God had been calling me to do. After going through my first weekend in 2006, I had the idea of doing a retreat on the island, but I did not have the courage. I made excuses instead of plans. During the time between going to the church retreat and going back to serve, I was going through many trials and being tested with my faith, family, friendships and finances. I was failing many of the tests, but I was remaining faithful and continuing to answer God's call in my life. There were many times when I fought with my family and my friends and struggled with my finances, but my faith continued to grow as I attended church, led a youth group and FCA, and prayed for the opportunity to serve on the church retreat. Even so, when the call to serve on the church retreat finally came, I had no idea what God would do in my life.

I will not share everything that happens on the retreats because I hope people will go to the church retreat and experience what God has in store for them. It is different for everyone, but they follow a model that invites the Holy Spirit to lead, and lives are changed as a relationship with Christ is forged.

While on the retreat, my roommate for the weekend was a guy named Noah. He had a similar background as me, and when he introduced himself, he shared that he was allergic to alcohol and that when he drank, he broke out in handcuffs. We were instantly friends.

One night, while on the church retreat weekend, Noah and I were talking about how awesome it would be to have a retreat for guys in recovery. He shared that he had been having a vision of doing a retreat in a place on the water, even describing a large marsh. He had no idea about the island, but he was describing it perfectly. I started to tell him about the island and went to my phone and pulled up a picture. "That's it!" he said. We began to pray and make plans.

We formed a team of six men to plan the first retreat. We decided to invite guys down to go fishing and share testimonies, sing worship songs, and get closer to Christ. We invited people from AA who did not go to church or have a relationship with Jesus. We did not want to preach to the choir. We wanted to reach the lost and broken, so we invited the addicted and the homeless. We decided to call it Fishers of Men after the scripture where Jesus was selecting the disciples, and He told them, "Come and follow Me, and I will make you a fisher of men." We planned to reel men in by offering a weekend of fishing and fellowship. Each man would invite others to come and share a testimony.

There was a terrible storm the day of the retreat, and we considered postponing. One of the team members said we were going to the island come hell or high water, so we showed up. There was an incredible rainbow that appeared on the way to the island, letting us know that we had made the right decision.

I was disappointed that none of the guys I invited came, but Noah showed up with a truckload of guys, eleven in all. One of them was Tim, who was invited by a brother from church named Bob. When Tim arrived, he was a disheveled mess. His hair was in a braid that was falling apart and hanging down his back. His teeth were all gone, and he was starving physically, spiritually, and emotionally. When the Holy Spirit overcame him on the island, Tim couldn't speak without tears streaming down his face. After the island, he went to a long-term recovery program. He put on weight, got his hair cut and his teeth fixed, and looked twenty years younger a year after coming to the island. His restoration was incredible, and he came back the next year to share a testimony.

Another of Noah's rescues was Al, who arrived drunk, detoxed on the island, and said a prayer on Saturday night that blew us all away.

Then, there was Dave, who was on the brink of suicide and had left a note at Noah's church that said he needed help. Noah's pastor asked him to go check on this man, and he went to visit him the day he was coming to the retreat. After speaking with him for about thirty minutes, Noah convinced Dave to join us. It was a pretty bold move by both of them. They had only known each other for a half hour, and something clicked. God was at work, for sure.

We were all overcome by the Holy Spirit that weekend. On Saturday night, Burt shared his testimony about losing his daughter to addiction and suicide. He searched for God's grace and found solace in Romans 8:38–39 (NIV): "For I am convinced that neither death nor life, neither angels nor demons, neither the present nor the future, nor any powers, neither height nor depth, nor anything else in all creation, will be able to separate us from the love of God that is in Christ Jesus our Lord." After Burt shared, we offered prayer, and the men broke down one by one. Chains were broken, and lives were set free. One man named Bill had lost a child as well. It was incredible to see the impact of God moving on the island and into the hearts of the men who came. Those of us who came to serve were fulfilled with much more than we could have ever given.

One of the projects we did on that first weekend was to build the crosses and erect them on the beach on the east side of the island. It was at this spot where Tim knelt, prayed, and felt the Holy Spirit and his life was changed forever. At the end of the weekend, we anointed each other with oil and left as the Fishers of Men.

The next year was set, and Hurricane Sandy came the week we had scheduled the retreat and actually moved the beach away from the dock by a good thirty feet. According to the neighbor, there were eight-foot waves crashing on the beach. Trees were down, and pieces of the neighbors' docks covered the beach. There were actually just enough pieces to stretch our dock to the new shoreline moved by the hurricane!

Something else pretty neat happened where we had put the crosses from the prior year. The sand that was moved from the west side of the island where the dock was located was now piled up on the east side by the crosses. It filled in a fifty-foot area, which became a perfect spot for us to have bonfires and a place to gather by the crosses. There was also a set of twelve steps that washed up on the shore, and we just laid them by the dune near the crosses and called it the stairway to heaven. The steps were used later and fit perfectly to access a gazebo we built from the beach after another storm washed away another section of the sand. I have seen the sands move many times, but God always makes a way to access the island.

After pushing back the second weekend, many of our guests and team members couldn't make it to the island. Noah had a work appointment and had to leave for most of Saturday. Tim shared an awesome testimony, then fell off the pier, tore a ligament in his knee, and had to leave. By Saturday night, there were only eight of us on the island, and Noah and I were feeling pretty discouraged. One of our new team members was about to share when another new guy stopped him abruptly. He said God just prompted him to share this verse with us. It was Romans 8:38. Immediately, the Holy Spirit hit us, and the hairs on our arms stood straight up. We were the only two from the prior year when Burt shared that verse. There was no way for anyone to know but God. He gave us a message at that moment, and we knew the retreat was exactly as He planned, not as we planned. The six men who came were impacted greatly.

The next day, as part of our Sunday homegoing, we went to a nearby church to share testimony and our weekend song. The pastor shared the sermon on Romans 8:38–39. He also had no way of knowing about this verse. Some might say this is a coincidence, but the pastor at the church closest to the island was my wife's good friend and our sponsor for the church retreat. She was assigned to the church just before our first retreat. This church welcomed us with open arms, and we have been welcome ever since.

The retreats have continued, and there are many stories of redemption and restoration to share. It was about 2016, and the Fishers of Men really expanded. I attended more recovery meetings and invited more and more men to come to the retreats. The numbers grew to thirty-three and then up to forty-four. One fish I couldn't reel in was Chuck. I kept inviting him every year. Sometimes, he would assure me he would come, but he always bailed with some excuse or just ignored my calls when it was time to go.

Once the kids went to college, our focus shifted from FCA to the Fisher of Men and paying for college. Just before my son graduated, we were having a particularly bad run at the office. We were just barely getting by again and wondering how we were going to put the kids through college. We had just paid off the rentals we had purchased when they were infants, and this was a big relief, but then we took out lines of credit to pay for college and other expenses. We also refinanced the house and the office building to reduce our monthly debt load. While these moves helped us, we still were struggling from time to time, depending on how sales went for the month.

One day, a local pastor who had a lot to sell came to the office. They had been negotiating with a local developer but were not able to put the deal together. The downturn in the market had hurt them as well, and they had to sell the lot to keep the church going. I told them I would help them sell the lot for no commission. It took a few months, but we got the deal together. When I brought the folder back from closing, Leigh asked me where the check was. I told her I had agreed to sell the lot for no commission, and she got a sick look on her face. She then told me she was counting on that closing to pay bills. It was the only settlement we had that month. I could see she was worried, and I told her that God would provide. He always does. She went to her office and cried.

The next day, I received a phone call from a developer who had one hundred and twenty acres to sell, and they wanted to sell quickly. The sale price was $1.2 million, and I listed it that day. As soon as the listing agreement was signed, I called the farmer who was renting the ground from the developer, and he said he would be right there to sign the contract to buy the farm back. This farmer had sold the land to the developer for 2.5 million when the market peaked in 2005. Six years later, the developer was struggling, as most were, and had to liquidate the property. The developer could have called the farmer directly, but they called me instead. My commission was over $70,000.

If you don't believe in God, it doesn't make sense. My faith tells me that God always provides, and He does. I believe that because I sold the lot for the church for no commission, God blessed us with something greater. Luke 6:38 (NIV) says, "Give and it will be given to you. A good measure, pressed down, shaken together, and running over, will be poured into your lap. For with the measure you use, it will be measured to you." We had always given when we had extra, but when we gave when we didn't have it to give, that is when God blessed us the most.

We started a new initiative at the office called "Our Mission of the Month." We started giving a portion of every closing to a different cause each month. Our agents would pick the cause, and we would give a check at our sales meeting. Ever since we have implemented this giving initiative, we have not lacked financially. God has continued to bless us as we put both of our children through college and were able to flip some homes and sell some properties that we have had for many years.

I decided to run ads for realtors in the "help wanted" section of a local newspaper, and at one of the agent interest meetings, I met Ryan. He stayed after the meeting, and we talked for a couple of hours, but hardly about real estate. We spoke about the good things God had done in our lives. He shared stories of his involvement with the men in Teen Challenge and mission trips to help impoverished people in Jamaica. I shared with him about the retreats on the island and the FCA rallies at the high school. We were instantly friends, and he became a top-producing agent in our firm.

He then invited me to go to Jamaica on a mission trip. I had heard about this trip and had actually helped support people to go. Ryan's family owns a building supply company, and Ryan heads up a construction project in Jamaica every year. He and his family have been going there for over twenty years to witness and share the love of Jesus. Typically, there are seventy or so people who attend this trip. Many are high school students who travel to schools doing music and skits about Jesus. In Jamaica, Jesus is welcome and taught in the public schools.

When I went in 2015, the construction project was to build a home for Bev, who lived under a bridge in Ocho Rios and was addicted to crack. Ryan would go under the bridge to witness to people, and he had met Bev there. He would pray with her and asked her about committing her life to Jesus and getting baptized. She told him it was too hard to follow God while living under the bridge. Ryan made a deal with her that he would build her a home if she would follow Jesus and get baptized. Ryan took me under the bridge to meet Bev, and I have to admit that I wondered if she would follow through and stay sober once the house was done. We spent all week building Bev's house, and I helped to buy rugs and housewares and anything she needed.

There was a young man named Adam who came every day just to help us, and we connected. He did not ask for anything, but we would give him lunch; he was happy just to do something good for someone. There were two small children who came to the house to watch and help every day, as well. They had a stick with a wheel on it and used it like a toy. My friend Tom, who was the soccer coach and helped start FCA in the high school, brought the used soccer balls from local high school teams and gave them to the kids in Jamaica. We would go to the boys' prison to give testimony and play soccer with the inmates. I asked him for a soccer ball to give to the two kids who came every day.

One day, while working on Bev's house, a construction truck came and unloaded a forty-yard dumpster full of trash on an empty lot in the community where we were working on the house. I couldn't believe they would just dump this construction debris in the middle of a city block. It was scrap lumber and drywall, empty five-gallon buckets, and other leftover material from one of the resorts that was being built in Ocho Rios. I was amazed that within hours, every piece of debris was picked up by the residents as they came one by one to use the items in their homes that were literally shacks on a hillside. Bev's house was basically a seventeen-by-twenty-four shed with a seven-by-seven bathroom and a concrete floor, yet it was one of the nicest in the neighborhood. I had a new appreciation for the blessings I had in my life and how good our life was in America.

We went under the bridge and brought Bev and her belongings to her new home. I watched as Ryan led her there and then to get baptized. He did his part, and now it was time for her to follow through. Bev detoxed and went to church every week after we left. She met a man in church and got married. She asked Ryan to walk her down the aisle.

I did not return to Jamaica for five years, but when I finally did, we got to see Bev, and she was dying of cancer. Shortly after our trip in January 2020, Bev passed. Unfortunately, Ryan could not attend her funeral because of the COVID-19 pandemic. While it was sad to lose her, we knew she was in heaven, as her faith never wavered, even while facing death.

CHAPTER 13:

Going Deeper

After a few years of doing the retreats, I was feeling encouraged by God to offer baptism to the men on the island; yet, just like the call to have the rally at the school, I made excuses and did not offer the invitation. I felt that God wanted me to do this, but I didn't feel worthy or qualified. I was not a pastor. I did not have any special training. Then again, I remembered that my baptism was spontaneous and by an FCA staff member and coach, not a pastor.

I had been wrestling with this during one retreat in particular, and while walking with a young man named John, he asked me to baptize him. I still doubted and told him that I was not a pastor and that we could get one to do it for him. He said specifically that he wanted me to do it. We made plans to do the baptism on Sunday after we returned to the island from church.

That Saturday night, I made the invitation, and two other men asked to be baptized. When I came home, I was so excited that I told my pastor. He reprimanded me, asking by what authority did I baptize them. I explained that Matthew 28:19 (NIV) says, "Go and make disciples of all nations and baptize them in the name of the Father, the Son, and the Holy Spirit." He was visibly disturbed by this, and a couple of weeks later, he gave a sermon in which he expressed his concerns but then admitted that the Scriptures do not say to go to seminary and get a degree and then go baptize people. It just says, "Go!" He never really gave me his blessing privately, but he told the whole church to go and make believers and baptize them, so I kept going.

I will never forget when we were having all of this discussion about baptism, and my daughter, Hailey, asked me to baptize her in the river behind our house. When I asked her if she was sure, she replied yes and said she wanted to do it right then and there. I was so happy for her and her commitment to Jesus. She has stayed sober her entire life. Knowing that she is much like me in her looks and personality, she has abstained, fearing that she would end up just like I did. Not to say that she has been perfect, but she graduated from college and became a special education teacher. We have often butted heads because we are both so stubborn. She is full of life, and she lights up a room. Sometimes, we have to tell her to dim it down a bit! She is wonderful and loving and fights for the underdog.

Noah moved to the Carolinas and quit coming to the retreat, so Burt and Sam really stepped up to help out more. Among the new guys who came were Karl, Steven, Jake, Paul, John, and Ron.

Karl, I met at the Thursday night meeting I have attended since I got sober. I had known him from the country club, and he was a real close friend of Vaughn, who had worked on my boat twenty years ago. We knew of each other but were not close. He was just out of rehab and was working on attending ninety meetings in ninety days. He was dedicated, determined, and willing to do whatever it took to stay sober. I invited him to come to the retreat that night, and he accepted the invitation. Prior to rehab, he had been drinking a box of wine a day. He was drinking wine because the liquor had gotten out of control. He had been to one rehab already, and he thought he could control wine better. Karl's life was a mess. He is an electrician and contractor, and his business was struggling. He was drinking all day long and taking pills as well. He was staying home alone and drinking in his office. He had a strained relationship with his wife and daughters. He was on the verge of losing everything.

Just before his second trip to rehab, Karl's best friend died from cirrhosis of the liver. While at his funeral, he was a pallbearer and was so drunk he could hardly stand up. A week later, he fell in his home office and hit his head. His wife took him to the hospital, where he stayed for a week. His blood alcohol content was so high, and his liver function was so poor that his body was shutting down. He had gained weight from alcohol bloat and could hardly walk. He had to learn to walk again and went from the hospital to rehab. He came on the retreat about four months later, where he gave his life to Christ.

Right after that fall retreat in 2016, we decided to have two retreats every year, one in the spring and one in the fall. At the spring 2017 retreat, Karl got baptized; and at the next retreat, he shared his testimony and also shared it publicly. His transformation and confidence in Christ grew tremendously. He began attending our church regularly and started playing drums in the praise band with Leigh Ann.

Shortly after Karl joined, the guitar player quit the praise team, then the bass player quit shortly thereafter. Leigh was discouraged. The praise team was shut down for a couple of months, and the church was not the same without live music. We looked and looked for a guitar player, and finally, I asked Leigh Ann if I could make a post on Facebook to find someone. Jerry, a friend who used to come over to play cards, replied. He had struggled with addiction and had been away to Teen Challenge to get his life together. He had been home for a little while and had been leading worship with Teen Challenge. Since the band was coming back, I decided to give the bass a try. I have been playing with the praise team church for more than four years now.

Jerry came on several retreats but continued to struggle. He went back to Teen Challenge in Michigan and was doing great. I went to his graduation and met Donald, who adopted Jerry as family. He had given up his home to turn it into a church and moved into his parents' basement next door. We stayed up for hours, sharing our faith. Jerry had connected with great, godly people and started working with a large real estate team. He was very successful and driven, and he received awards for his production. For his two-year "soberversary," he came back to visit and stayed with us for about ten days. We had a victory tour, as this was the longest period of sobriety he had ever accomplished. He gave the message at Teen Challenge, and we had a two-year celebration at our home group. He visited with family and friends, and everyone commented on how well he was doing. When he went back to Michigan, I felt as if he finally got it and had no worries for the first time in our friendship.

A few weeks later, I got a call from Donald, who informed me that Jerry had died from an overdose. I was shocked and completely numb. My number was the only one Donald knew. I told him I would reach out to his family. Calling Jerry's mom was one of the most difficult things I have ever done. This news was devastating because it was so unexpected. It is so tragic how one slip can end a life so quickly, especially after a period of sobriety.

Karl, however, continues to be a success story. He has been such a great friend and has helped me selflessly with so many things. Sometimes, we argue like brothers, but more often, we laugh together, encourage one another, and pray together. Karl just celebrated seven years of sobriety and continually helps guys in the program.

A couple of years ago, Karl got a call from his sister about a guy named Jason, who was married to her co-worker and just getting out of rehab. We met him at a meeting and took him to the island. Then we invited him to church, and he came. When Jerry left for Teen Challenge, Jason started playing in our band. He just celebrated two years of sobriety and has been doing tremendously, and he continues to attend the retreats and reach out to guys in recovery.

The aforementioned Ron was invited by Burt. He had just moved back to Delaware from California, where he ended up addicted to meth and ultimately living in a trash enclosure in LA. He was invited to move into a sober living house, got sober, and was saved by the grace of God. He went from a place of despair, hopelessness, and homelessness to many years of sobriety and a beautiful home that he has opened to men in need. He has had several roommates who have come to the island.

One such roommate, Nick, was a former Pennsylvania state heavyweight wrestling champion. He had legs like tree trunks and was a gentle giant. Following a back injury, he was prescribed pain pills. This eventually led to a full-blown heroin addiction. Nick came to Lower Delaware to get a fresh start. He met Ron and started working for him. Ron always opened his home to guys working through recovery, and Nick moved in with them. Being the great Fisher of Men that he is, Ron brought Nick to the island retreat, where I was paired up with him as Nick's best friend for the weekend. He slept in this little red pup tent where his head and feet were pushing on the sides. We called him "Big Nick Little Tent" and had a great time all weekend fishing, crabbing, and jet skiing.

On Saturday evening, we have a special dinner with Communion. On this particular weekend, monarch butterflies flew around us and landed on us as we ate. It was after dark, and I had never seen butterflies flying at night, let alone landing on people. Something great was happening. We passed the butterflies around and took some pictures as some of the guys questioned, "Frank, how did you make this happen?" I replied that only Jesus could make this possible. It was surreal, but more importantly, Nick was all ears as he listened intently to the men share their faith and recommitted his life to Jesus. He also got baptized that weekend. It was incredible, and we could see God smiling on Nick.

After a while, Nate went back to Pennsylvania and relapsed. His car ended up in a ditch, and his life was a mess. He called Ron, and immediately, he drove six hours to Western PA to pick him up and bring him back to Delaware. Nick got it back together and moved back in with Ron. He was working and scheduled to come on the next retreat. It had been a year since he had been on the island, and there was a hurricane in the forecast.

Ron called me the week before the retreat and asked if we were going to postpone the weekend because of the forecast. I told him I was going to pray about it until Wednesday and then make a decision. As I prayed, a verse came to me. Proverbs 3:5 (NIV): "Trust in the Lord with all your heart and lean not on your own understanding." I said, "Okay, Lord, we will have the retreat." After watching the forecast some more, I thought I should pray further. While I was praying, a very clear answer came to me. It was not an audible voice that I heard, but my thoughts became clear and undeniable that God said, "Do you trust Me or the weatherman?" This was on Tuesday. When Wednesday came, and the weather channel was claiming an eight-foot tidal surge, I asked God again, "Are You sure we should have this retreat?" It was clear that I heard His reply: "I told you twice already. Now, you have work to do."

Nick and some others did not come because of the pending storm. Ron called Nick and tried to get him to come, but he had hurt his back and decided to stay home and rest. The hurricane went west around the peninsula, and as we watched the clouds and storm in the distance, we were not affected and had a beautiful weekend. The sun was shining, and we had many men come to Jesus and get baptized.

Right after we took the men off the island and returned to clean up, Ron got a phone call that Nick had overdosed and passed away the night before. First, we cursed and cried in disbelief. One minute we were on top of the world, excited about the breakthrough that happened in the men who came to the island. The next minute, we felt defeated and asked ourselves, "What's the point of what we are doing when we have just lost a brother?"

As we gained our composure and told the other guys who were still on the island what had happened, I stopped to talk to Karl in the spot where Nick's tent had been the year before. I told him that we had to do more and more men to reach. The enemy took Nick, but we were not going to give up. We were going to kick the devil in the nuts for this one. Just at this moment, two butterflies circled around us, and I felt the Holy Spirit come over us. It was hard to hold back the tears as I drove home and wrestled with God about losing Nick. I pulled up to my home about midnight, and there was a monarch butterfly on the entry door of our home. I have been in and out of that door thousands of times, and never before or never since has there been a butterfly on the door, not to mention that it was midnight. Only one other time in my life have I seen a butterfly at night, and that was during dinner with Nick on his first retreat.

God kept blessing us with more retreats and more men. One of them was Chuck. When Chuck got out of prison, we would talk periodically and get together to go on the boat or for a jet ski ride. I could sense the regret he had when he would come over and look at his old house next door to ours. He had lost everything.

Finally, his son, Aaron, had written him off and was not speaking to him. I had not seen Aaron for quite some time, but he was making his way in the world and had started a pressure-washing business. He had dropped off some business cards at our office, and he looked really good. He had matured and seemed to be on the right track. We spoke briefly about Chuck, and I could tell that he wasn't pleased about where his dad was heading.

I kept reaching out to Chuck and inviting him to meetings and church. He came on the retreat and started coming to church here and there. He also started to attend our recovery group regularly, but there were also times when he would not show up and not answer the phone, and we knew he was off to the races again.

Out of the blue, I stopped by his house, and he was drinking heavily, among other things. I asked how he was doing, and he instantly broke down and told me that he had lost his reason to live, as his son was still not speaking to him because of his addiction. I responded that if he kept doing what he was doing, he would keep getting what he was getting.

As he cried out, I asked him if I could pray with him. He poured out the beer and sat in my truck. While I was praying, I asked him if he wanted to pray with me. He just kept pleading with God that he wanted his son back. Before we could even say amen, my phone rang, and Aaron was calling me. I felt the Holy Spirit come over us as I answered the phone, and Chuck and Aaron spoke. I left Chuck that day and assured him that God was real and was listening. It was time to get right with Him and get his life together. I did not want to visit him in the hospital or prison or hear about him dying of an overdose.

A week went by, and Chuck called me and asked what he needed to do to get saved. I explained that he needed to believe in his heart and confess with his lips that Jesus is Lord. Chuck asked how he could do that and know that he was sincere. He said he had lied so much throughout his life that he did not know if he could even be honest. I said that was the most honest thing I had ever heard him say. I also shared that God would know if he meant it or not. Chuck said the Sinner's Prayer that day and gave his life to Christ. He was committed to God and church and recovery meetings. He even gave his testimony on a retreat.

I got a chance to reconnect with Aaron and share with him how God had delivered him from Tourette's. Aaron admitted that he was struggling with drinking and smoking pot. I advised him to seek God and start praying. I shared some scriptures with him, and he took notes. I prayed with him and invited him to come to the island, where we took a boat ride and jet-skied through the marsh behind the island. It was a fantastic time, and we created memories I will never forget. Aaron admitted that he did not know how good he had it as a kid but wanted to have a great life and was willing to do what it took to achieve his goals.

I saw Aaron a month or so after our trip to the island while I was busy on the phone. He looked great and was excited to see me. I motioned that I was on the phone, and he said he would catch me later. Sadly, later never came.

Chuck was one month shy of celebrating one year of sobriety when I got a call on Sunday morning, October 13, 2019, from his now-wife, Christine. It was before church, and a state trooper had just come to their house to inform them that Aaron was killed in a car wreck along with two of his best friends, who were brothers. I immediately went to see Chuck.

We cried all day, and then his mom and sister arrived, and they cried some more.

At first, I was angry with God; then, I became pissed at the devil. I know God had better plans for Aaron. He and his buddies were drinking and getting high when he lost control of his car. They struck a telephone pole going one hundred miles per hour. The car rolled for three hundred feet, and they all died at the scene.

We had Aaron's funeral at our home, and around three hundred people came. It was torrentially raining and so sad. I gave the eulogy and shared stories about Aaron growing up next door and Chuck coming to know Jesus and getting sober. Aaron was so proud of Chuck, and it was just heartbreaking to lose him at the best time of Chuck's life when he was giving and doing for others, enjoying sobriety, and living a good life. It was so tragic, and Chuck was filled with grief and remorse, but the only consolation was that he was sober when Aaron passed, and their relationship was better than ever. Aaron's friends got in their trucks and smoked their tires in front of our house in his memory.

The next day, we took the flowers from the funeral to the crash site where the three boys passed away. We put up the flowers and went looking for a necklace that Aaron used to wear all the time. While we were walking around the yard where the crash happened, his girlfriend was adamant that she wanted a sign that Aaron was in heaven. A minute after she made this statement, a rainbow appeared. There was no rain that day. There were not even many clouds in the sky. It was an incredible moment as God showed us that He has Aaron in

His hands, and we prayed with Tina and the rest of the people at the crash site.

CHAPTER 14:

Reel 'Em In...

One day at our office, I met a guy named Luke in our parking lot at the office. I was having a bad day as we were struggling to keep up with the maintenance on the rental properties we were managing. Here was this guy with a dump truck, and I asked him what he did with the truck. He replied that he could do cleanouts, repairs, or anything we needed, so we gave him some jobs to do. He did a good job for us, so we gave him more work. As I got to know him better, he told me how he used to be a pagan and was in recovery from a meth addiction. He was trying to turn his life around. I invited him to the island, but he gave me excuses and said he was too busy.

On Mother's Day 2019, he called me drunk. He had a gun and was threatening to kill himself because he didn't have any money and couldn't take his wife to dinner. He had done some jobs and turned in some bills that we had not paid yet, so he was upset with me as well. I told him I would bring him some cash right away if he would put down the gun. When I got to his home, he showed me that he was struggling with more than just a cash shortage. He was smoking pot to keep himself calm, he said. His home was a mess and falling apart after having caught on fire. He, his wife, and his daughter were living in a camper while he was trying to rebuild his home.

I told him I would help him put his home back together, but he would have to do his part and come to meetings and church. I would get volunteers and donations and do whatever I could to help him, but he would have to stay sober. I could not ask people to give time and money to help him if he were buying weed and alcohol.

He did his part, and we did ours. Ryan was a big inspiration to me in this project, the way he invested in Bev and how she came out from under the bridge to Jesus. I asked him to help, and he was there. Luke came to meetings and church faithfully for about ninety days, so we got to work. The Fishers of Men came through big time. Karl helped him wire the home, my new neighbor, Vince, helped him with a discount on the insulation, and Leigh and I paid the bill. Many friends and organizations gave money to pay for materials. About ten of the Fishers of Men showed up to hang drywall. Luke was back in his home around Thanksgiving. He finally came on the retreat and has attended every one since. He has been coming to church and meetings faithfully, and he and his wife have been praying together. His daughter has even been on the youth version of the church retreat, and they finally went once the COVID-19 restrictions had been lifted. His wife and daughter recently spoke at his anniversary about the man he has become. They are proud of him and how he has grown to lead his family in the way of Jesus.

Luke has been paying it forward and helping many people, including Ryan, with local charity building projects. We are also planning to take Luke to Jamaica with us when we can go back.

About six months prior to him attending the church retreat, I found out Luke and several other brothers in the Fishers of Men were using medical marijuana. I felt betrayed and heartbroken as these men were claiming to be sober and leading recovery meetings. I prayed about what to do and could not let it go without taking action. Two of the guys were working for our real estate company, and I gave them an ultimatum: either give up the weed or find work elsewhere. One of the guys left our company the day after the ultimatum. I explained that I could not, in good conscience, send him leads and give him business when I knew he was using the money to buy drugs. Luke kept an open dialogue. While he was angry at my ultimatum, he did not shut off communication. The other friend left our group chat and quit speaking to me, accusing me of being closed-minded. They both kept attending church but had no intention of quitting smoking weed. Then his church retreat weekend finally came, and God spoke to him. He gave it up and has not gone back. I challenged another brother who was using weed to give it up as well, and he unfriended me, left our group chat, and quit speaking to me, accusing me of being closed-minded.

In the spring of 2020, the enemy attacked in a way no one saw coming. COVID-19 happened, and people reacted in fear. They stayed home, and restaurants and businesses shut down, and many facilities stopped allowing recovery meetings.

A new guy named Cory came to the recovery meeting. He was young and intelligent, a college graduate and high school valedictorian. He had a good job and a beautiful wife. He was also addicted to pills and alcohol. He had lost the trust of his family and was on the verge of losing his wife. He came in ready for a change and willing to do whatever it took to get back on track. He listened intently, shared his struggle openly, and made progress. He was primed and ready for our spring weekend on the island. The church retreat weekends were canceled, and businesses and everything were shut down. I was shocked that even church services were canceled.

Many people were telling us to cancel the island retreat, and I was considering doing so until Cory told me he would go no matter what. We had a smaller group, but it was just as powerful. God still moved, and many great things came from this weekend.

When we arrived, our usual parking area on the point across from the island was occupied, so we parked up and down the road. One neighbor left notes on the cars, called the police, and berated me in front of everyone when we were leaving to go to church. I kept trying to reason with her, but there was no reasoning; she was livid and did not want us parking on the road. She called the county to have our cars towed and signs put up in the right of way. I reached out to the neighbor who usually lets us park on his property on the point across from the island. I had been trying to acquire his lot ever since we bought the island and offered to purchase it again. He said he was not ready to sell but would keep us in mind.

In spite of the issues with COVID-19, parking, and decreased attendance, our time in fellowship was incredible. God smiled on us all weekend, and we were able to attend our first visit to the Church by the Bay. Since all of the area churches were shut down due to COVID-19, they began meeting at the county dock while holding an outdoor drive-in service. We were able to connect with more people, and the churches became more unified. The Church by the Bay made national news as they had continued to meet as one even after the COVID-19 restrictions were lifted.

Our fall retreat was better attended, and one of my childhood friends came to the island for the first time. Walter was all in from the beginning. He had struggled with addiction his entire life, going to countless rehabs, detoxes, and prisons.

Before we have dinner on Saturday evening of the retreats, we have a special including Communion, modeling what Jesus taught at the Last Supper ceremony, and then we present the men with a cross made of nails. It represents what Jesus commands us to do in loving and serving others. The men who come for the first time are served and loved just like we were on our first weekend. I will never forget the tears that flowed down Walter's cheeks as he felt the love of Jesus at this sacred moment. After the retreat, he began coming to church, attending our reunions, and staying connected. He has been serving others ever since and has been sober for nearly three years.

Another success story is Ike, whom I met while selling real estate. He moved to Delaware from Pennsylvania and had twenty years in AA before he was hit by a car trying to help someone change a tire and was prescribed pain pills. His addiction to pills kept him down and spread to his wife as well. Christmas day of 2019, he threw out all of the pills and went into his room to detox for six days. He was using a cane and a wheelchair. Doctors said he would be on pain management for his entire life and that he would never walk again without assistance. He came to our spring retreat and gave his life to Christ. He got baptized and is now serving faithfully in church. He is walking tall without a cane or a wheelchair. He rides his motorcycle now and has a boat. My favorite thing is to hear him sing "Waymaker" while walking through Walmart. He is on fire for Jesus and always fishing!

CHAPTER 14:

Fisher of Men Foundation

In April of 2021, we had our largest turnout for an island retreat, with over fifty men scheduled. There was rain in the forecast. We decided to move forward and rented a tent.

A few months prior to the retreat, I met a young man named Brian, who asked me to be his sponsor after speaking at a meeting. We spent a day together, and it turned out he had his real estate license. He was living in a recovery house after having recently gone to two different rehabs and overdosed two times.

After only a week of sponsoring him, he was kicked out of the recovery house for using and selling OxyContin. I met him at a local convenience store where a lot of drug dealing occurs. He was just sitting there nodding out, high as a kite. I asked him if he wanted a ride to rehab or if he wanted to stay on the street. He agreed to go back to rehab, so we drove to a twenty-eight-day facility about twenty miles away. While we were driving, he kept nodding out, and I kept shaking him awake to answer questions for the intake person who was on the phone. I was scared that he was overdosing, but I finally got him to rehab.

I stayed with him until they took him in, only to get a call on my way home that he had left the facility. Without hesitation, I called the police and informed them that this twenty-four-year-old addict had left the rehab heavily intoxicated and in a town where he knew no one after telling me that he did not care if he lived or died. The police found him and took him to the hospital for a twenty-four-hour lockdown and evaluation, after which his parents came to get him.

He promptly fired me as his sponsor since I had called the police on him, but I just kept reaching out. I found out a week later that he had overdosed again, this time in his home. His brother did CPR until the paramedics showed up and gave him Narcan, and he was saved once again.

After his latest overdose, I reached out again, and this time, he was receptive to coming on the retreat. He arrived having just started on Suboxone, and he nodded out most of the first night and the next day. Many guys came to me concerned about him. I just told the guys to keep encouraging him, loving him, and praying for him. The second night there, we were under the tent as the rain poured over us. We offered to pray for anyone who needed it. One by one, man after man sat down, and we prayed for at least an hour, maybe two. As each man sat down for prayer, we could feel the presence of God and the Holy Spirit pouring over us heavier than the rain.

During this time of prayer, Brian was heavy on my heart and mind. I kept thinking, *I hope he comes for prayer.* I did not see him in the tent, but it was dark. When we had prayed over everyone who was standing in the prayer huddle, I asked if there was anyone who would like prayer, and Brian responded from the corner, "I could use some prayer." When he sat down,

I cried out to God to deliver him from his addiction and bring healing to him. Every man in the huddle was pleading right along with me, and Brian stood up as a different person. He was brighter. He stopped nodding out the rest of the weekend. He was smiling. God intervened, and he was delivered from an opiate and fentanyl addiction. When he went home, his parents could see a difference in him. He has stayed off of heroin and oxy since then, but he has continued to smoke weed and is not currently speaking to me because I kept challenging him to quit. He continues to underestimate what God can do for him, but I know he will be delivered from all substances in His time.

But another miraculous thing came out of that weekend. As we went to our tents for the night and continued to get rained upon, I began to pray about building a structure on the island to accommodate everyone during the retreats, no matter what the weather.

We still had an issue with parking, as the neighbors were not happy with all of the vehicles up and down the road during the retreats. The property across the creek from the island had been abandoned for some time, and we could usually park there, but not always. I would periodically ask the neighbors who owned this property if they would consider selling, as we really needed this space for access and parking. They always declined, but the property was really falling into disrepair. I would often cut the grass as it was overgrown and deteriorating. As we left the retreat, I spoke to a few men about building a structure on the island, and we prayed on the property where we were parked, claiming it in the name of Jesus. After we prayed, one of the men, who did not hear our prayer or know what we were discussing, walked over and gave me $600. He said God told him to give me this money. We had never taken any money for the retreats before; actually, no one had ever really offered because we would just all pitch in and bring whatever we needed. I was surprised, but I accepted his donation and told him I would pray about what to do with the money.

When I got home, I reached out to a friend who had been a source of inspiration and encouragement to me over the years. He had started a few nonprofits, and I asked him about the process. He encouraged me to start a 501c3 nonprofit and said he would donate some seed money once we were up and running. And so it was that we started the Fisher of Men Foundation and set up our first meeting to select our board and begin plans for the building. The week we were meeting, I got a call from the neighbor on the point property across from the island. He was ready to sell, so I made him an offer, not knowing where the money would come from.

We had our meeting to select our board. As we assembled to pray over what we were about to do, the wind picked up over the water, and it reminded me of a song that had just come out. We could all feel the presence of God come over us as the wind and Spirit blew in. It was an incredible moment as we felt His blessing on what we were doing. We selected our board and wrote our articles of incorporation and bylaws.

The next morning, I received a call from the neighbors that our offer was accepted, and they were giving us two additional lots as well, a double portion. Now, how to pay for all of this was the question. I knew God would make a way. I was really surprised when Leigh agreed to move forward with the purchase. We had just spent years working on our finances to get to a place where we were more financially stable, and now I was asking her to spend over half a million dollars just so we could have a place to park for the retreats. I was surprised, but I knew it was God's will when she did not hesitate to say yes. I asked several people to partner in the project, and one of our agents and an old friend went in with us.

My wife and I donated $5,000 and opened the bank account. Within a week of starting the foundation, our brother Mark made a few phone calls and raised over $15,000. We had raised $20,000 just by telling people about what we wanted to do on the island. We met with a church to discuss making a donation, and the question arose: what would happen if I lost my religion and decided not to host the retreats anymore? We agreed to lease our weeks on the island to the foundation, but then God did something even greater. The partner who had bought one-third of the island several years prior decided to sell his shares. He was willing to give the foundation a very fair price and hold financing, so now we have ownership and so many more weeks available to use the island for our ministry.

At the very next retreat, after we started the foundation, we were blessed with the most incredible sunset to the west, and when we turned to the east, there was a rainbow over the island. It was confirmation that God was blessing what we were about to do.

Leading up to this weekend, Leigh Ann's dad, Maynard, was not doing well, so we called our kids to come see him. As hard as it was to see him struggle, I knew God was working on the circumstances and that he would hang on until after the retreat. You see, I had invited my son, Zak, to come many times, but he never would. In God's perfect timing, He would have it work out that Zak would be seeking a relationship with Jesus as he had just begun attending church and a men's group. There were over fifty men attending the retreat, and when the offer for baptism came up, Zak responded. It was an answer to years of prayer and patience as Jesus became a priority to my son.

My friend Jake was also baptized that weekend. Jake had been struggling with alcohol, prescriptions, and anxiety. He had lost his mother at a young age to cancer. She was a very godly woman who was a member of their church choir. Jake then lost a sister to cancer, as well, and became very angry toward God. He had wrecked cars and relationships. On his first retreat six months prior, Jake reconnected with Jesus and picked up his guitar after years of not playing. When we returned from the retreat, he joined our praise team and has been playing with us ever since. He later lost his father but has not lost his faith. Jake has grown tremendously in his faith and has become a huge supporter of the Fisher of Men. He has been doing some fishing as well by inviting men to the retreat.

Meanwhile, God just kept working out every obstacle to the retreat house. He took care of the parking issue and quadrupled the availability, and more donations kept coming. My long-time friend, the one who said he would give some seed money, gave us $40,000. Remember Walter, my childhood friend who gave his life to Christ on the island a few years ago? His sister and family gave us $35,000. The church we met with gave us $10,000. In total, we raised over $100,000 in less than six months. God was providing in a big way.

As we began the process of designing the building, we settled and started to work on the point property. It was in extreme disrepair, and we went way over budget, but we were blessed to sell the two additional lots that came with the package. Our brother Ike loves Deal Island, and after selling his home in PA, he decided to purchase the lots so he would have his own piece of Deal Island. Ike is so excited about what is happening with the Fisher of Men that he thinks the next revival in our country is going to start in little old Deal Island. I pray he is correct.

As the work on the point progressed and we planned for our spring retreat, another rainbow appeared over the island. This time, it was a double rainbow. It was amazing to see God's promise cover the island for a second time in six months. Our spring retreat was another incredible turnout. Chuck came again but slept most of the time. I could tell that he was coming down from a binge, and his heart was not in the weekend. He had told his wife that he was coming on Thursday but did not show up until Friday and left early on Sunday. He was mad at me because I called him out for lying around all weekend. In spite of Chuck being down, it was a fantastic weekend filled with brothers connecting and sharing faith.

In our small group was a guy named Dave and another named James. Dave struggled off and on for a while but acknowledged Jesus and kept calling. One night at three in the morning, I got a call that Dave had jumped on a cargo train and was headed to Texas. He has relapsed many times since we met, but he keeps calling me and coming back to the island. Earlier this year, he was baptized, and he is currently sober.

CHAPTER 15:
Nothing but God

When James came to the island, he was facing serious charges of assault on a police officer while he was on parole. He was struggling with isolation and addiction prior to his arrest. He met Byron, who had been coming to the island to celebrate recovery and who always helped in the kitchen with Paul while he was waiting for bail. Byron had been previously incarcerated for a sex offense and violated his probation by picking his daughter up from school. As a registered sex offender, he is not permitted on school grounds. Even as we were praying for Byron to be released, he was in prison, fishing. James was his cellmate, and he invited him to the island retreat.

So, to recap, I met Joe at AA and invited him to the island; Joe invited Paul from HALO, the homeless shelter where he was volunteering; and Paul became sober, came to the island, gave his life to Christ, and completed the Journey of Hope program at HALO. Paul then came to the island eleven more times and invited Byron, whom he met in Celebrate Recovery. Byron, in turn, invited James, whom he met in a jail cell in Jessup prison. Only on the island is it perfectly normal for a registered sex offender to invite a stranger who violated parole for assaulting a police officer to experience a new way of life. John has since invited Ken and Matthew, and Ken has been baptized.

James came with the weight of the world on his shoulders. Over the weekend, he opened up and connected with Jesus and his new brothers in Christ in an amazing way. You could see the walls of his tough exterior break down, and his eyes fill up with tears of joy, just like Joe, Paul, and Byron. I cry every retreat when I see the goodness of God and the Holy Spirit go to work on all of us.

Another guy named Trent came, as well. He had faith but also had extreme anxiety. When he went home, his wife could see a difference in him. He really did not have a struggle with addiction, but he has not had a drink since that weekend, almost a year ago. There were also two young men, Justin and Leo, who were baptized. Both of them came to church and meetings for a little while, but both relapsed. Leo is in prison, but Justin just came out of rehab and is doing better. It is easy to see that relapses happen once church and meeting attendance stops.

Chuck kept struggling with his son's death and addiction, but he kept coming to the island. In the fall of 2022, he was finally all in. From the start of the weekend, he was engaged and participating. We cried tears of joy and grief over his son, Aaron, and over our brother Jerry dying. He was helping do whatever was needed. He connected with Pastor Fred, and when he came home from the island, he regularly attended the chapel where Pastor Fred preached and even joined a Bible study. He shared messages with the Fisher of Men group chat that he was no longer angry with God for taking Aaron but glad that Aaron was with Jesus.

I was so excited that he was finally at peace with God. Unfortunately, it was short-lived. It wasn't long before Chuck quit going to church and started using heavily again. It was like he wanted to die. One night, he called me at two in the morning from his dad's house. He said he was ready to go to rehab and wanted me to take him. He felt like he had overdosed and was afraid he was going to die.

It was freezing cold outside, and when I got to the house, he was walking around high as a kite, not making any sense of what he was saying. He was a walking skeleton. I pleaded with him to get in the car, but he refused, so I drove away. I got a mile down the road and called him. I told him I would be back to get him, but if he refused to get in the car a second time, I was going to call the ambulance because he had told me he overdosed. I came back again, only for him to walk back into his dad's house, so I called the ambulance. The police always come when there is a suspected overdose. His dad woke up and let the police in. At this point, Chuck was hiding in the bathroom, refusing to come out for medical attention or to go to the hospital. He was cussing at me for calling for help. It was clear the drugs were talking and directing his steps.

When he finally came out of the bathroom and agreed to let the paramedics do an assessment, one of them searched the bathroom and found the crack pipe and needles he was using. I gave it to the police, but they said they could not arrest him because it was only paraphernalia and there were no drugs. Every time Chuck saw me standing there, he started ranting and yelling at me to get out of his dad's house.

Needless to say, we did not speak for a while. A couple of months went by, and Christine told me he was still using and his health was getting pretty bad. He never truly recovered from that drug binge, and his organs were shutting down, so he called hospice care. I stopped by his house to see how he was doing, and his legs were so swollen from fluid that he could hardly walk. It was clear that he was not going to last long, so I went home and just cried with my wife. I knew there was nothing more I could say or do but just love him.

I decided to visit him three more times that week, and I could see that he was getting worse every day. Every time I sat with him, I would ask him if I could pray for him, and he would say, "Absolutely." We would pray and cry as we both knew what was coming. Christine said he was still leaving the house every day, and it was obvious he was still using. She caught him in the car one night in the driveway, and he tried to hide the pipe between his legs.

The last day I went to see him was Easter Sunday, and I knew he was close to leaving us. I asked him if he knew where he was going, and he told me, "Yeah, it is going to be hot…" We both laughed. Then I told him that he was like the thief on the cross and he was going to heaven even though he did not deserve it. We prayed and cried again and told him I loved him, and he said the same. He died that night in the back of the barbershop where he had been using regularly.

At Chuck's funeral, the Fishers of Men came out to show love and support to the family. Pastor Fred gave an incredible tribute to Chuck; we sang with gratitude, and as we were singing, all of us were crying. We stood up in unison and could feel the presence of God lift us up at that moment, and we knew His grace was greater than Chuck's sins.

The next day, Dan called me and said he had never been touched by God or felt the Holy Spirit until that moment, and he knew without a doubt that God was with us there. When he got to the car, his wife asked, "What was that?" Dan replied, "That was nothing but God."

CHAPTER 16:

Building an Ark

Throughout the fall of '22 and into the spring of '23, we built the Fisher of Men building. The outpouring of support has been incredible. The guys who attended the retreats showed up big time. Steven estimated the pour would take one thousand eighty-pound bags of concrete. I called concrete companies to see if there was a way to pump the concrete 1,100 feet from the mainland to the island. There was no way. We had to transport all 80,000 pounds across the creek to the island. We rented mixers and equipment and called on everyone we could find to volunteer. We had fifty volunteers show up on a Saturday, but due to equipment failure and getting stuck in the sand, we could not unload the concrete until Sunday and rescheduled the pour for Monday. We had another fifty volunteers come on Labor Day and got the pour done. We had one bag of concrete left over. *Jireh.* The weather was perfect, and even though we were tested with equipment issues and not having volunteers lined up until Sunday for the rescheduled pour on Monday, God made a way. The rest of the building has been an incredible amount of work, but nothing like the pressure of time and weight involved in pouring that concrete.

We held our first retreat on the island in the new building in the spring of '23, and fifty men came. We worshiped God fully, and everyone came closer to Jesus that weekend. Three men were baptized: David, who is doing well; Rex, who helped tremendously with the electrical work; and my new best friend for the weekend, Kenny from PA, who just celebrated one year sober. My favorite part of every weekend is hearing the men share what the weekend meant to them and what they are going to do about it. There are always tears of joy from the men who have just experienced the presence of Jesus.

On a Fisher of Men weekend, we expect a transformation in the lives of struggling men that can only occur through divine intervention. There have been many miracles and lives changed in this forty-eight-hour experience. On every retreat, it is expected that God will do in a weekend what hasn't been accomplished through years of struggling with rehabilitation, prisons, homelessness, grief, and recovery programs. Many men have been set free from a lifetime of addiction and slavery to sin through the Fisher of Men retreat. Men who attend the retreat are introduced to a new way of life and bond with brothers who will walk beside them as they overcome whatever personal battle they are facing.

I can't wait for the next weekend and pray this book will help just one person find recovery and Jesus. If it is God's will, we will be able to expand our ministry and host many more weekends. We have recently opened a Christ-centered recovery home and hope to start building homes to help the men with employment and build a future. We have hosted two couples' weekends and are planning women's weekends and family events as well.

While every weekend is a mountaintop experience, the process of recovery takes time and work. We encourage the men to stay in contact with each other, get involved in church, and find a recovery group that feels like home. Step work is key as well.

Jesus can heal anyone in a moment, but we have a choice to keep following His way or go back down our own path. Salvation is freely given and happens in a moment, but sanctification is a process that requires action. As with the prodigal son, no matter how far away we have run from our Father, when we turn around, He will run to us and welcome us back with open arms.

If you or anyone you know is struggling with addiction, depression, or suicidal thoughts, please reach out to us through our website, FisherofMen.us. We will do our best to get you connected with a recovery program and schedule a time to attend a Fisher of Men retreat. You are not alone! Jesus and the body of Christ are with you.

Also, reach out to your local church and keep seeking. Remember, not all churches are perfect because they are full of broken people. Everyone needs healing, or we would not need a Savior. Salvation is a decision that is made in a moment, but sanctification is a one-day-at-a-time process.

> *But seek first his kingdom and his righteousness, and all these things will be given to you as well. Therefore do not worry about tomorrow, for tomorrow will worry about itself. Each day has enough trouble of its own.*
>
> — Matthew 6:33–34 (NIV)